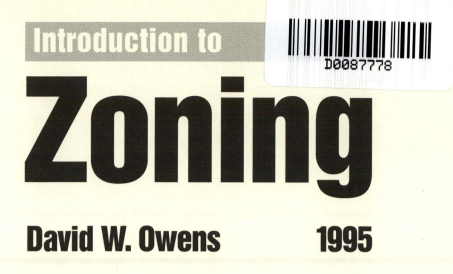

Introduction to
Zoning

David W. Owens   **1995**

INSTITUTE *of* GOVERNMENT
The University of North Carolina at Chapel Hill

THE INSTITUTE OF GOVERNMENT of The University of North Carolina at Chapel Hill is devoted to teaching, research, and consultation in state and local government.

Since 1931 the Institute has conducted schools and short courses for city, county, and state officials. Through monographs, guidebooks, bulletins, and periodicals, the research findings of the Institute are made available to public officials throughout the state.

Each day that the General Assembly is in session, the Institute's *Daily Bulletin* reports on the Assembly's activities for members of the legislature and other state and local officials who need to follow the course of legislation.

Over the years the Institute has served as the research agency for numerous study commissions of the state and local governments.

Michael R. Smith, DIRECTOR

FACULTY

Stephen Allred
A. Fleming Bell, II
Frayda S. Bluestein
Mark F. Botts
Joan G. Brannon
Anita R. Brown-Graham
William A. Campbell
Margaret S. Carlson
K. Lee Carter, Jr.
Stevens H. Clarke
Anne F. Davidson
Anne M. Dellinger
James C. Drennan
Richard D. Ducker
Robert L. Farb
Joseph S. Ferrell
Cary M. Grant
Milton S. Heath, Jr.
Cheryl Daniels Howell

Joseph E. Hunt
Kurt J. Jenne
Robert P. Joyce
Jeffrey S. Koeze
Patricia A. Langelier
David M. Lawrence
Charles D. Liner
Ben F. Loeb, Jr.
Janet Mason
Richard R. McMahon
Laurie L. Mesibov
David W. Owens
John Rubin
John L. Saxon
Roger M. Schwarz
Thomas H. Thornburg
A. John Vogt
Michael L. Williamson

© 1995
Institute of Government
The University of North Carolina at Chapel Hill
∞ This publication is printed on permanent, acid-free paper in compliance with the North Carolina General Statutes.
Printed in the United States of America
ISBN 1-56011-275-1
❸ Printed on recycled paper

Contents

Introduction   1

1. Overview: Principles and Tools of Zoning   3

History and Evolution of Zoning   5
Other Tools for Regulating Land Use   11

2. City and County Zoning Jurisdiction   13

City Jurisdiction   13
County Jurisdiction   14
City Extraterritorial Jurisdiction   14
Individual Local Agreements   18

3. The Form and Content of Zoning Ordinances   19

Use Districts and the Zoning Map   19
Use Restrictions   24
Dimensional Requirements   25
Other Typical Zoning Requirements   27

4. Overview of the Zoning Process   29

Types of Zoning Decisions   29
Zoning Hearings   30
Zoning Boards, Staff, and Other Parties in the Zoning Process   31
Public Access to Meetings and Records   33

5. Legislative Decisions: Adoption, Rezonings, and Text Amendments   35

Notice of Proposed Amendments   36
Hearings   37
Protest Petitions   38
Waiting Periods   39
Zoning and the Comprehensive Plan   41
Spot Zoning   42
Contract Zoning and Conditional-Use District Zoning   44
Judicial Review   46

6. Quasi-Judicial Decisions   49

Special Rules for Decision-Making Process   49
Special-Use Permits   54
Variances   55
Appeals   57
Judicial Review   57

7. Administrative Decisions and Zoning Enforcement   59

The Zoning Officers   59
Duties of the Zoning Officers   60
Zoning Enforcement   60

8. Special Consideration for Existing Development   67

Vested Rights   67
Nonconformities   70

9. Constitutional Limits on Zoning   73

Due Process   73
Equal Protection   75
First Amendment   76
Taking   77

10. Statutory Limitations on Zoning Powers   83

Appendix 1: Zoning Statutes   89

City Zoning Enabling Statutes   89
County Zoning Enabling Statutes   101
Other Key Statutes   112

Appendix 2: Further References on North Carolina Zoning Law   117

Index   119

Introduction

Zoning has become one of the most visible and important functions of local governments over the past seventy-five years. These days, land-use management decisions stir tremendous public interest. It is not uncommon to hear vigorous citizen debate on zoning decisions confronting a community: Should multifamily or commercial development be allowed on this site? How will this rezoning affect traffic congestion? Is there any way we can protect this historic neighborhood or these natural resources? Will this zoning decision stifle economic development? What will this do to my property values? It is not surprising that citizens pack zoning hearings, pressuring local governments to "get it right" when making zoning decisions.

Most critical zoning decisions are made by citizens serving on government panels rather than by professionally trained local government staff. City council members and county commissioners, for example, decide whether or not to rezone a parcel. Board of adjustment members decide whether to grant a variance to zoning regulations. Planning board members advise on rezonings and may make final decisions on special approvals required for some developments. These decisions can have a tremendous impact on landowners, their neighbors, and the future quality of the entire community. Both the citizen board members making these decisions and the citizens attempting to influence the choices must fully understand the legal requirements for zoning in order to do their jobs fairly and effectively.

This book is intended to provide a clear, understandable explanation of zoning law for citizen board members and the public. It is not a detailed legal treatise on zoning law; rather, it is an introduction for citizens new to these issues or a refresher for those who have been at the zoning business for some time. Those who need more detailed information may check the references cited in Appendix 2. The reference works cited there, many by Institute of Government colleagues Richard D. Ducker and Philip P. Green, Jr. (now retired), are a valuable and rich resource.

Each chapter of this book deals with a distinct aspect of zoning. The book can be read in its entirety, or the reader can turn to a question of particular interest. The table of contents or the index will give the reader quick directions to topics of interest.

This book also contains occasional sections that examine landmark zoning cases in more detail. These are introduced by this symbol ▦ and are offset from the regular text.

1   Overview: Principles and Tools of Zoning

How nearby land is used makes a powerful impact on people. As North Carolina's woods, farms, and small villages of the past century have made way for cities, suburbs, industrial parks, and shopping malls, communities have had to adjust to the change. Citizens find themselves wrestling with difficult questions. They ask, Is this the kind of place I want to live, where my children will want to live? How can we encourage quality growth and development while keeping the things that make our community a special place?

Some questions address the big picture: How can we provide safe, decent, and affordable housing for all citizens? How can we protect the quality of our air, our water, and natural resources? How can we make our cities attractive, efficient, and livable? Others are much more immediate and personal: What will the new strip development along the bypass do to my business downtown? How will a fast food place on the corner affect my neighborhood? Can I put a mobile home out behind the homeplace so I can care for my ailing mother?

Because the way one person uses his or her land can so deeply affect neighbors and the broader community, it is not surprising that the role of government in this area has grown over the past seventy-five years. These days, local governments prepare plans and studies to better understand the implications of such decisions. Citizens talk about the directions they want their community to go in. And communities adopt regulations that limit what people can do with their land. These regulations, while adopted to benefit everyone by promoting the common good, do limit our personal choices. Finding the right balance of individual and community interests is a demanding job, one fraught with controversy, difficult choices, and a host of legal rules.

While local governments use a host of tools for land-use planning and regulation, their principal tool is zoning. Almost all urban areas and many rural counties in the United States use zoning ordinances to regulate how land is used and developed. Zoning can be used to separate incompatible uses of land, preserve the character of communities, protect natural resources, or promote economic development. Indeed, the emergence of zoning as the principal way we collectively deal with issues of land use and development led U.S. Supreme Court Justice Thurgood Marshall to note in a 1974 case that zoning "may indeed be the most essential function performed by local government, for it is one of the primary means by which we protect that sometimes difficult to define concept of quality of life." This book explains what zoning is and how it works, with a focus on North Carolina.

The basic principle of zoning is simple: zoning creates a number of different districts, or "zones," in a city or county, each of which sets specific rules on how the land in that district can be used. For example, a district set aside for residential land uses may exclude businesses and industries. A local governing body sets forth the specific rules and zone boundaries in the form of a zoning ordinance. Zoning ordinances, in addition to specifying land uses permitted in each zone, often also set detailed standards on how permitted uses may be carried out. For example, zoning ordinances often contain instructions on "setbacks," the minimum distances new buildings should be set back from the street. Other kinds of requirements, or "development standards," commonly found in zoning ordinances include the minimum number of parking spaces businesses must have for their customers, the maximum sizes of advertising signs, standard lot sizes or building heights, and landscaping requirements.

Property owners in a residential neighborhood rely on local zoning ordinances to protect the economic value of their homes and the family character of their neighborhood. Owners of vacant land use zoning to determine what they can build and sell there, a decision that often has a substantial impact on the value of the land. Local governments rely on zoning to predict what kinds of urban services, such as roads, water and sewer lines, and schools, will be needed, as well as when and where they need to be installed. The cost of providing these urban services affects the taxes everyone pays. Planning ahead by using zoning can help keep costs and taxes under control.

Zoning is one of the most visible and controversial activities of local governments. It is not surprising, then, that a substantial body of law has developed detailing how zoning shall be carried out. Virtually all zoning decisions are made by local governments, both in North Carolina and nationally. Technically, however, zoning power is a state government power that has been delegated to cities and counties. This is significant because it means that the state legislature passes laws that set the legal framework within which local governments adopt, amend, and implement their zoning ordinances. State statutes "enable" or authorize local governments to adopt zoning ordinances. While local governments decide whether or not to have zoning and what the content of the zoning ordinance will be, the process they must follow in making those decisions is set by state law.

The state legislature imposes a number of special requirements on how zoning power may be exercised. These requirements ensure that the zoning process includes broad public notice and discussion of the policies and standards proposed. The courts also restrict zoning activity, mostly by protecting the rights of persons affected by zoning decisions. The chapters that follow discuss these legal requirements and restrictions on zoning.

History and Evolution of Zoning

In the late 1800s and early 1900s, local governments in the United States began to enact ordinances to regulate where certain kinds of businesses could locate and how big certain kinds of buildings could be. Early examples include an 1885 Modesto, California, ordinance regulating the location of laundries; ordinances regulating building heights in Washington, D.C., in 1899 and in Boston in 1904; and a 1909 Los Angeles ordinance restricting the siting of industrial plants. The Modesto ordinance is notable not only because it may be the earliest example of a city regulating business locations, but also because it shows just how controversial such regulations can be. For years people have argued whether the Modesto ordinance had the noble purpose of minimizing the harmful impacts of commercial laundries on residential areas or the ignoble purpose of racial discrimination against the Chinese immigrants who were the proprietors of most of the regulated laundries.

In 1916 New York City developed the nation's first comprehensive zoning ordinance. The construction of a subway system and the development of high-rise construction had created a hazardous situation. Buildings were so close together and contained so many people that inadequate ventilation and fire safety were serious problems.

In addition to these concerns, the increasingly crowded city was facing complaints generated when businesses, industries, and residential areas were located so close to one another. As in Modesto, California, in New York separation of the social classes played a role in motivating the move to adopt zoning. Proprietors of exclusive shopping stores along Fifth Avenue complained that low-income workers from nearby garment factories were crowding the sidewalks and driving away prosperous customers, prompting the shopkeepers to call for zoning restrictions to move the factories to a more distant location. To address all these issues, the city adopted a comprehensive zoning ordinance.

The problems with incompatible land uses, traffic, noise, congestion, and loss of amenities were certainly not confined to New York City. Neither was the desire to keep certain types of industry, business, and housing (and perhaps the people who lived and worked in them) in their "proper" place. As the nation shifted from a rural to an urban population, people were increasingly affected by their neighbors' land uses. In 1800, less than 4 percent of the nation's population lived in cities. By 1920 that figure had passed 50 percent, and the national drive to develop new ways to deal with land-use management took off.

Other cities around the country soon adopted the New York zoning model. The U.S. Department of Commerce promoted the zoning concept by encouraging all the states to grant to their local governments the power to adopt zoning ordinances. In 1922 the Department of Commerce, under the leadership of then-Secretary Herbert Hoover, published a model state zoning-enabling code. The national movement to adopt zoning ordinances got a big boost in 1926 when the United States Supreme Court ruled the zoning concept constitutional.

In the period after World War I, the national trend to adopt zoning quickly took hold in North Carolina. Many cities had by then already adopted some rudimentary land-use regulations, but most regulations addressed only such issues as the location of individual buildings considered nuisances or hazards, such as wooden buildings in the center of cities. In North Carolina, local governments have only those powers granted to them by the legislature, and those powers must be exercised in the manner set forth by state statutes. In 1923, the General Assembly gave cities the authority to adopt zoning ordinances. By the late 1920s a dozen of the larger cities in the state had zoning ordinances.

In the earliest days of zoning, it was unclear whether the courts would uphold use of this new regulatory tool and, if so, what legal constraints the courts would impose. In 1931 the North Carolina Supreme Court resolved many of these questions in an early landmark decision on zoning. This colorful case involved feuding neighbors, a stubborn landowner, and an unyielding city government, all engaged in a five-year-long battle over the use of a single lot in Elizabeth City. This fight produced four state supreme court decisions and was ultimately resolved by a special act of the legislature.

The land involved in this case was a fashionable residential block adjacent to the downtown area of Elizabeth City, then a town of about 10,000 people. Mr. A. L. "Ab" Aydlett resided on the corner of this block nearest downtown. Aydlett's brother, Mr. E. F. Aydlett, a prominent local attorney and perhaps the most influential political figure in the region, owned the Southern Hotel, located across the street from this corner lot (see Figure 1, opposite). In the spring of 1928, E. F. Aydlett spent some $100,000 (a considerable sum in 1928) to renovate the hotel so it could compete with a new rival hotel in town. Ab Aydlett then proposed to put a new gas station on his corner lot across the street. The neighbors, how-

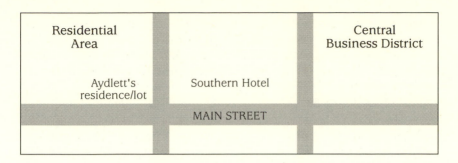

Figure 1. Aydlett's lot and surrounding properties.

ever, strenuously objected and convinced the city council in July 1928 to adopt an ordinance prohibiting gas stations in this residential block.

This was far from the end of the matter. In February 1929 Aydlett erected a wooden shack on his lot, right next to the street and his neighbor's property. His next-door neighbor complained to the local paper that Aydlett was just trying to block his views and make the neighbors' property as undesirable as possible in retaliation for their stopping his gas station project. In April the city council, by a four-to-three vote, refused to amend the gas station ordinance to allow construction of a station on this lot. Undeterred, in August Aydlett demolished part of his residence, moved the rest to the side of the lot, and began construction of his gas station on the corner without the city's approval. The opinions quoted on the front page of the August 2, 1929, edition of a local paper, *The Independent*, could have been from people in many contemporary zoning disputes. "It's my property, I'll do with it what I please," said Aydlett. The city's response: "The thrift and enterprise of all the people of the city have contributed to the upbuilding of your property and you have no right to devote your property to a purpose that would be destructive of the property values of other residents." Both sides agreed the matter would soon head to court, although it is doubtful they knew how long their case would stay entangled there.

The city promptly issued Aydlett a criminal citation for violation of the gas station ordinance. On September 10, 1929, Aydlett won his first legal battle when the trial court declared the gas station ordinance unconstitutional because it did not apply citywide and because it exempted existing gas stations. The fact that Ab was represented by his brother, E. F., and that the trial court judge was E. F.'s son-in-law, no doubt aided his case. The city appealed the decision and got an injunction to prohibit work on the station while the case was on appeal.

At the same time the city headed on another tack. In August 1929 the city resurrected its moribund planning commission and asked it to develop a zoning ordinance. The planning commission examined newly adopted zoning ordinances in Raleigh, Durham, High Point, Rocky Mount, Richmond, and Norfolk. In early September the commission proposed a zoning ordinance for Elizabeth City. On October 1 the city held a public hearing on the proposed zoning ordinance and not a single person appeared to oppose it. The big news of the day was not the zoning hearing, but the announcement that the region's first talking picture equipment was to be installed in the city's Carolina Theater later in October. On October 7, 1929, the city adopted its first comprehensive zoning ordinance. The ordinance put Aydlett's lot in a business zoning district, but one that did not allow gas stations. So the great gas station battle continued.

On April 9, 1930, the North Carolina Supreme Court ruled that the city should not have been granted an injunction to enforce the gas station ordinance after Aydlett had been acquitted on the criminal charge. So Aydlett began work the next Monday to finish building his gas station. But the city was in court by Monday evening to get the work stopped. By Wednesday, the station was half built but the court ordered work halted. Both sides again appealed, with the mayor telling the local paper, "We'll fight this thing to the last ditch."

The parties were back in court in May 1930. This time Aydlett had hired plumbers to install lines to his station and they had tunneled under the city sidewalk to do so, prompting yet another city suit. The parties were back before the same judge, the son-in-law of Ab's brother and attorney. The city attorney and judge promptly got into a heated dispute that nearly landed the city's lawyer in jail. The judge opined, "The City doesn't give a rap whether or not Mr. Aydlett tunnels under a sidewalk. I see this case as nothing at all but spite work on the part of the City. I shall not prosecute any such case in my court. The City ordinance may be valid, but I'm going to dismiss the case. I have no patience with the small methods and tactics of the City in fighting Mr. Aydlett." When the city attorney responded that he took this to mean he should not bring any more indictments for violations of the law, the judge threatened him with jail for contempt of court. The incident led to a spirited but unsuccessful effort to unseat the judge in the June 1930 elections. It did not, however, deter either side from continued legal battles. For example, when Aydlett asked for city approval to remove the curbs to install a driveway into the station, the city denied approval. Aydlett tore up the curbs anyway, and the city took him to court in 1930 for that as well. In any event, the structure was completed in 1930, but it sat vacant for another three years while the legal battles continued.

When the second round of cases made it to the state supreme court in 1931, the issue was compliance with the zoning ordinance. The court issued three opinions in this last stage of the case. In the first, it concluded that injunctions could be used to enforce zoning. In the second, the court said injunctions could be used to prevent interference with city

Figure 2. In 1931 in *Elizabeth City v. Aydlett*, the court upheld a zoning-ordinance prohibition against future filling stations, even though existing stations were allowed to remain. Two years later, however, the owner of the site successfully got local legislation passed allowing his station. It was built, and operated for many years. The Southern Hotel is in the background.

sidewalks, trees, and street lights. In the third and most important of these cases, the 1931 landmark opinion *Elizabeth City v. Aydlett*, the court upheld the constitutionality of zoning in North Carolina. The court also ruled that a land use (in this instance, for gas stations) could be completely prohibited from a particular zoning district and that new uses could be prohibited without requiring similar existing uses to be closed. Both of these points were essential to the legal and political viability of zoning and the case cleared the way for widespread adoption of zoning by North Carolina cities.

Even though Elizabeth City won the court case, it still eventually lost the battle of the use of Aydlett's lot. Having lost with the city council and in the courts, Aydlett was more successful in the legislature. In the spring of 1931, before the supreme court's ruling upholding zoning, the General Assembly had almost short-circuited the whole matter. A local bill to exempt the gas station from the city's zoning passed the House of Representatives but was killed in a Senate committee. (A local supporter of the bill claimed it lost only because Ab's station was leased to Gulf and one of the Senate committee members had a cousin who worked for Texaco.) In 1933 the matter got to the General Assembly a second time. This time the legislature adopted a local bill allowing gasoline service stations in any

Elizabeth City zoning district that allowed "retail stores, shoe shops, barber shops, pressing shops, restaurants, confectioneries, offices, hotels, theaters, assembly halls, news stands, wholesaling or jobbing"—which, not coincidentally, just happened to describe the uses allowed in the district that covered Aydlett's lot. Aydlett was finally able to open his gas station.

The gas station operated on this corner in downtown Elizabeth City for some thirty years. The structure, shown in Figure 2 (page 9), was eventually converted to other business uses. Sixty-five years later, the building is still being put to commercial use in its present incarnation as a health food store.

By the 1960s most of North Carolina's mid- and smaller-sized cities and towns had adopted zoning ordinances. Zoning came later to rural areas. While a few of the most urbanized counties had local legislation authorizing zoning, counties were not granted general zoning authority until 1959, and it was not until the 1980s and 1990s that many counties adopted zoning. By 1994, 23 of the state's 100 counties had more than 50,000 people living in the portions of their county outside of cities. More than two-thirds of the state's counties had at least 20,000 noncity residents. This population growth fueled the public demand for land-use management in places well beyond the state's largest cities. Currently more than 350 cities and 65 counties in North Carolina have adopted zoning ordinances.

Zoning is now widely used in North Carolina and around the nation. Yet we live in a time when there is great interest in protecting private property rights and great skepticism about governmental regulatory programs. What explains the endurance—and even expansion—of zoning? For one, zoning has become our principal tool for protecting property values. By using zoning to prevent incompatible uses from being too close together and by providing a degree of predictability about future land uses, local governments provide a degree of stability to the land market that property owners and developers both find reassuring. Other mechanisms, such as developers instituting private restrictive covenants and citizens filing nuisance suits against their neighbors, are far less effective means of accomplishing such goals. Zoning is a valuable tool in other areas as well. It can help foster economic development, protect aesthetic and environmental resources, facilitate the more efficient provision of public services, and protect and enhance the character of a given community.

Over the years, North Carolina's enabling legislation for zoning has evolved in several ways, becoming broader in some areas and more specific in others. First, the state has provided local governments with the authority to use more regulatory tools for land-use management. For example, local governments can now use *conditional-use district zoning* to tailor regulations to individual projects and can regulate and protect historic structures and neighborhoods. Second, the state mandates state-level protection for a few kinds of facilities to keep local land-use regulations from unduly restricting them. These include manufactured homes, family-care homes, hazardous waste and low-level-radioactive-waste sites, and facilities with state ABC permits. These limits are discussed in more detail in Chapter 9. Third, the state has imposed rigorous procedural requirements on local land-use regulation. Fourth, the state has mandated that local land-use regulations protect natural resources of critical importance, such as water supply watersheds and mountain ridges. In addition, cities or counties can and often do secure legislative approval of modest individual variations in the zoning power for their own local governments only.

Just as state legislation on zoning has evolved in character and complexity over the past seventy-five years, so have local zoning ordinances. Zoning ordinances of the 1920s typically created only three zoning districts, a residential, a commercial, and an industrial district. A modern ordinance may create twenty or thirty different zoning districts. Zoning ordinances increasingly include standards beyond the basic ones restricting land uses and building size and location. These days ordinances routinely set standards for off-street parking, landscaping, signs, storm-water control, mixed-use projects, and other aspects of development. Zoning procedures are also more complex, from public notice requirements to hearing processes. What was once a relatively simple ten-page document has transformed into a hundred pages of regulations with specialized terminology and arcane procedures that can be difficult for citizens, board members, and the staff to comprehend.

Other Tools for Regulating Land Use

While local governments use zoning as their principal tool to regulate land use, they often use other related ordinances as well for that purpose. *Subdivision control ordinances* regulate the creation of new lots or separate parcels of land, usually giving standards on how the new lots are laid out and what common improvements, such as roads and utilities, must be provided. *Building codes* regulate how new construction must be conducted, with standards for structural safety and for electrical, plumbing, and heating systems. *Housing codes* set minimum standards for the upkeep of residential structures. *Nuisance lot ordinances* set minimum standards to prevent lots from becoming overgrown or becoming repositories for unsightly and unhealthy collections of refuse. *Sedimentation control ordinances* regulate construction sites to keep soil from eroding. In recent years, some local governments have attempted to simplify ordinances such as these by consolidating zoning and other related ordinances into a single, unified *development ordinance.*

In addition to land-use restrictions imposed by government, private agreements such as restrictive covenants or deed restrictions can limit how land is used. For example, the developer of a new residential subdivision may establish restrictive covenants that set a minimum size for houses, limit architectural styles, or restrict where recreational vehicles may be stored on a lot. Such covenants are often more strict than local zoning requirements. Because they are private agreements between the seller and the buyers of the lots in that development, however, they cannot be enforced by the local government. Lot owners can sue to enforce the covenants—unless the covenants are illegal—but the local zoning enforcement officer does not enforce them. An example of an illegal covenant would be one that restricts sale of a house to buyers of a certain race. Whether a restrictive covenant is legal or not, its enforcement is a private matter, and the zoning officer is not involved.

2   City and County Zoning Jurisdiction

Once a city or county decides it needs zoning, how does it decide who zones what territory? The state may allocate zoning powers exclusively to either cities or counties. Alternatively, this power could be assigned to a state agency. Since many issues such as water and air quality protection and transportation need to be addressed on a regional basis, states can assign zoning powers to regional agencies, such as multicounty councils of government or special agencies covering metropolitan regions such as North Carolina's Triangle or Triad. Still, in North Carolina, as in most states, zoning remains almost exclusively the province of cities and counties.

As for the division of responsibility between cities and counties, city zoning generally applies inside of the city and county zoning applies outside of city limits. There are, however, two important variations on this rule. First, North Carolina cities have authority to extend their zoning to the urban fringe area just outside of the city limits. This is called *extraterritorial zoning*. Second, cities and the counties they are located in can agree to vary these standard arrangements; for example, a small city may ask a county to exercise county zoning within that city. This chapter will review the laws governing which local government has zoning jurisdiction for particular geographic areas.

City Jurisdiction

Cities have exclusive authority to adopt, amend, and repeal zoning ordinances within their city limits. If a city does adopt a zoning ordinance, it must apply it to all the land within its boundaries. Unlike counties, cities do not have the option of zoning only a part of their jurisdiction.

City boundaries change. When a city grows, it can absorb newly developing areas just outside its borders. This expansion of the city's boundaries is called *annexation*. In North Carolina, the state statutes have very detailed standards for when a city can expand through annexation. For large cities in North Carolina, for example, unless the land in question is being annexed by the request of the landowner, the area to be annexed must have a population density of at least two persons per acre or at least 60 percent of the land area must be subdivided into lots of five acres or smaller, among other standards. When the city expands its boundaries, the city must extend its zoning to cover the newly annexed land.

A transition provision in North Carolina General Statutes 160A-360 allows any county zoning that was in place prior to annexation to remain in effect for up to sixty days while the city holds the required hearings to amend its zoning ordinance. However, the county zoning automatically expires either when the city adopts zoning or sixty days from the day the area became part of the city, even if the city has not yet zoned it. Cities can start the notice and hearing process on the zoning amendment before the effective date of the annexation, so the change in jurisdiction and the application of city zoning happen simultaneously.

County Jurisdiction

In 1959 counties in North Carolina were given general authority to adopt zoning. Before then, only a few of the larger, more urbanized counties had gotten special authority to adopt zoning, and zoning in North Carolina was largely confined to cities.

These days many counties have adopted zoning ordinances. County governments in North Carolina have the option of zoning only a portion of their jurisdiction. A county can zone all of the noncity territory in the county or only a part of the county, or it can choose to have no zoning at all. Figure 3 illustrates which counties have full, partial, or no zoning.

If the county chooses to zone only part of its jurisdiction, each area zoned must be at least 640 acres, and must contain at least ten separate tracts of land in separate ownership. Counties may later add smaller contiguous acreages to a zoned area.

City Extraterritorial Jurisdiction

The way an area immediately outside a city is developed can dramatically increase the demand for city services, change the city's traffic patterns, and change its property values. In many instances such nearby areas will eventually be a part of the city and thus should be developed according to the city's regulations. Since 1959 virtually all North Carolina cities have had the authority to extend city zoning to the area immediately outside of their city limits. This area is called a city's *extraterritorial jurisdiction*, or ETJ. The extraterritorial area need not meet the same standards that are required for annexation in order to be included in a city's zoning ordinance, and areas covered by extraterritorial jurisdiction need never be annexed (though most eventually are).

Figure 3. By the early 1990s, two-thirds of the state's counties (shown above) and nearly three-fourths of its cities had adopted zoning ordinances. (Data from North Carolina Department of Commerce, Division of Community Assistance.)

Within the ETJ area, the city can apply all of its land-use ordinances—zoning, subdivision, floodway and sedimentation control ordinances as well as building and housing codes. Cities can also acquire open space and apply their community development and community beautification programs in an ETJ. A city cannot apply its general regulatory ordinances—such as nuisance lot or noise ordinances—to its ETJ, nor may it apply any land-use ordinance not also applied inside the city limits.

The maximum size of an extraterritorial area depends on a city's population. The larger the population, the larger the ETJ may be, with a maximum boundary of three miles outside the city limits. (See Figure 4.) ETJ

Population	Maximum Distance in Miles from City Limits
< 10,000	1
10,000–25,000	2
> 25,000	3

Figure 4. Limits of extraterritorial area for cities.

limits measure only from a city's principal boundaries. A city cannot extend extraterritorial jurisdiction to the fringe area around noncontiguous areas of the city (its *satellite annexations*).

A city can choose to exercise less than its maximum extraterritorial area. For example, it may establish jurisdiction extending one mile east

Figure 5. A city can extend its ETJ to part of the area around the city without extending it to the entire potential ETJ area.

of town because that is the direction of urban growth, while not establishing any extraterritorial jurisdiction on the west side of town. Figure 5 illustrates this sort of arrangement. If two cities are close enough together that their extraterritorial boundaries overlap, the boundary is set at the midpoint between the cities. (See Figure 6.)

State law encourages cities to use identifiable geographic features, such as rivers, roads, or rail lines, when setting the actual boundaries of extraterritorial areas. The boundary need not be surveyed, nor must it follow property lines. However, the boundary should be defined clearly enough that people can easily tell whether or not their property is within the city's jurisdiction. A very general boundary description, such as "one mile in all directions from city hall," would not be legally sufficient; boundary lines drawn on county tax maps would be.

It should be noted that a city's extraterritorial area boundary does not automatically change when the city's corporate boundaries change through annexation. If, for example, a city of 10,000 has adopted a one-mile ETJ area and the city subsequently extends its corporate boundaries by annexing out three-fourths of a mile, the ETJ boundary stays in the same place and the city then has an ETJ area of only a one-quarter mile. The city can later amend the ETJ boundary to add territory up to a mile from the new city limit, but it must again go through all of the proper steps to do so.

In order to exercise extraterritorial jurisdiction, a city must adopt an extraterritorial boundary map ordinance. Once a city determines its proposed new ETJ boundary, and formulates its extraterritorial boundary map ordinance, the city must set a date for a public hearing on the proposal and provide notice of the hearing to affected citizens. Notice of the hearing must appear once a week for two successive weeks, with first notice at least ten but not more than twenty-five days before the hearing. The city is not required to mail notice of the hearing on the ETJ boundary ordinance to individual property owners, but mailed notice must be provided when the city extends its zoning ordinance to the area. Therefore many cities hold a single hearing on the ETJ ordinance and the extension of their zoning ordinance and do provide a mailed notice of that hearing.

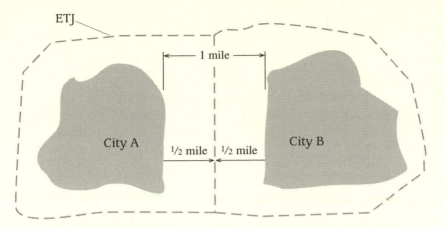

Figure 6. Where two cities' potential ETJ boundaries overlap, the ETJ boundary of each is set at the midpoint between the two cities.

In some situations, the city must receive county approval to establish or extend its extraterritorial jurisdiction. Within the first mile, county approval is required only if the county is already exercising all three land-use tools—county zoning, subdivision control, and building code enforcement—for that geographic area. For extraterritorial jurisdictions extending more than one mile from the city, county approval is always required. The county gives approval in a written resolution adopted by its county board of commissioners. There are no standards set for the county board to use in making the decision on whether to allow the city to have the ETJ. That choice is left to the good judgment and discretion of the county commissioners. The county commissioners may rescind their written approval, but they must give the city two years' written notice before doing so.

Once the city council has followed these steps, it may adopt the extraterritorial boundary map ordinance by a simple majority vote. After adoption, the city must file a copy of the adopted map of the boundary of the ETJ area with the city clerk and with the county register of deeds. This is the official copy of the new boundary that citizens can check to determine whether or not their land is covered by city zoning regulations. Of course, the city must also promptly move forward with an amendment to the maps in its zoning ordinance to apply zoning to this new territory, if that had not been done when the ETJ boundary map was being adopted. Just as when it annexes territory, when the city extends its ETJ into an area previously zoned by the county, the county zoning stays in effect for sixty days or until the city zoning takes effect, whichever comes first.

Finally, after a city establishes extraterritorial jurisdiction, it must provide for representation by residents of this area on certain city boards. Residents of the extraterritorial area do not get to vote in city elections

1. Prepare adequate boundary description.
2. Publish newspaper notice of public hearing.
3. Notify individual property owners in affected area.
4. Secure formal county resolution of agreement if necessary.
5. Adopt ordinance.
6. File copy of boundary map with city clerk and register of deeds.
7. Amend city zoning ordinance to add area to zoning map.
8. Appoint extraterritorial members to city planning board and board of adjustment.

Figure 7. Summary of steps a city must take to establish extraterritorial zoning.

and do not pay city taxes. However, the city planning board and board of adjustment have to be expanded to include residents of this area—or other county residents if there are not enough residents in the extraterritorial area itself. The county board of commissioners appoints county citizens to these city boards; if the county commissioners fail to make these appointments, the city council makes them.

Figure 7 provides an overview of the steps a city must take in order to establish or change its ETJ boundary.

Individual Local Agreements

Special legislation or local agreements allow exceptions to rules on geographic jurisdiction for zoning.

Cities commonly ask the General Assembly for approval to extend their extraterritorial jurisdictions beyond the limits described above. A fast-growing city with a population under 10,000, for example, may ask for the authority to have up to two miles of extraterritorial area. The legislature also can adopt special legislation setting respective extraterritorial boundaries in high-growth areas with multiple cities, as was done in Mecklenburg County.

Local agreements between a city and county may also create variations to the general jurisdictional rules. For example, a city can ask the county to apply county zoning within the city. Two nearby cities can agree to an extraterritorial boundary that is not midway between their cities. Such local agreements must be in writing, must be adopted by the governing boards of both governments involved, and must be consistent with the rules described in this chapter. For example, a county cannot agree to let a city with a population under 10,000 extend its extraterritorial jurisdiction more than a mile; only the General Assembly can amend that standard.

3 The Form and Content of Zoning Ordinances

A modern zoning ordinance can be an imposing document. The zoning ordinances for larger cities are frequently more than two hundred pages long. It is not unusual for even a small town's zoning ordinance to be fifty or a hundred pages long. To further complicate matters, each ordinance is unique—there is no standardized format, content, or even terminology for zoning ordinances in North Carolina. For example, a zoning district named "R-10" in one ordinance may allow single-family homes on 10,000-square-foot-lots, but in another zoning ordinance an "R-10" district may allow multifamily residential units at a density of ten units per acre. Such differences between one ordinance and the next, however, allow cities and counties to tailor specific provisions to address local needs and government policies. Despite the lack of standard formats for them, ordinances do typically address certain issues and contain some common features—elements found in most zoning ordinances.

Use Districts and the Zoning Map

While most city and county ordinances—from taxes to dog licensing—apply uniformly throughout the jurisdiction, zoning sets different standards for different parts of a jurisdiction. To accomplish this, a zoning ordinance must contain a map as well as detailed textual instructions. First, the text of the ordinance describes what is permitted in each district, what procedures have to be followed, and the like (see Figure 8, page 20). Second, a map places the land in the jurisdiction into various zoning districts (see Figure 9, page 21). This map is an official part of the zoning ordinance. Any changes in the map to move land from one zoning district to another, called a *rezoning,* is an amendment of the zoning ordinance and must follow all of the procedures required for zoning amendments.

Early zoning ordinances provided only a few broad zoning districts. Land was generally placed in one of three districts: a *residential district,* a *business district,* or an *industrial district.* These early ordinances also typically set these districts up as *cumulative districts.* That is, the residential district would be the most restrictive and no other land uses were allowed in them. The business districts would allow both businesses and residential uses. The industrial districts were the least restrictive allowing industrial, business, and residential uses. Figure 10 (page 22) illustrates the

CHAPTER 4   9-4-2

ZONING

DISTRICTS AND USES

9-4-1 DISTRICTS ESTABLISHED

All property within the jurisdiction shall be divided
into zoning districts with designations and purposes
listed in Section 9-4-2 (District Descriptions).

9-4-2 DISTRICT DESCRIPTIONS

(a)   General Use Districts

(1) Agricultural:

AG AGRICULTURAL DISTRICT

The AG, Agricultural District is primarily intended to
accommodate uses of an agricultural nature including farm
residences and farm tenant housing. It also accommodates
scattered nonfarm residences on large tracts of land. It
is not intended for major residential subdivisions. The
district is established for the following purposes:

a.   to preserve the use of land for agricultural,
      forest, and open space purposes until urban
      development is enabled by the extension of
      essential urban services;

b.   to provide for the orderly transition to urban
      uses by preventing premature conversion of
      farmland;

c.   to discourage any use that would create
      premature or extraordinary public infrastructure
      and service demands; or

d.   to discourage scattered commercial and
      industrial land uses.

(2) Single-Family Residential:

In the following districts the number refers to the
minimum lot size in thousands of square feet.

a.   RS-40 RESIDENTIAL SINGLE FAMILY DISTRICT

The RS-40, Residential Single Family District is
primarily intended to accommodate single family
detached dwellings on large lots in areas
without access to public water and sewer
services. The district is established to
promote single family detached residences where
environmental features (such as within water

4-1

Figure 8. The text of a zoning ordinance defines the use districts, development standards, and procedures to be used in zoning.

"zoning pyramid" that was established by these early cumulative zoning districts. The primary objectives of these early ordinances were separation of incompatible land uses and the protection of residential property values, both of which could be accomplished with this basic approach.

In the past fifty years this early arrangement of zoning districts has become substantially more complicated. Zoning ordinances now have more districts, with each district being more narrowly defined.

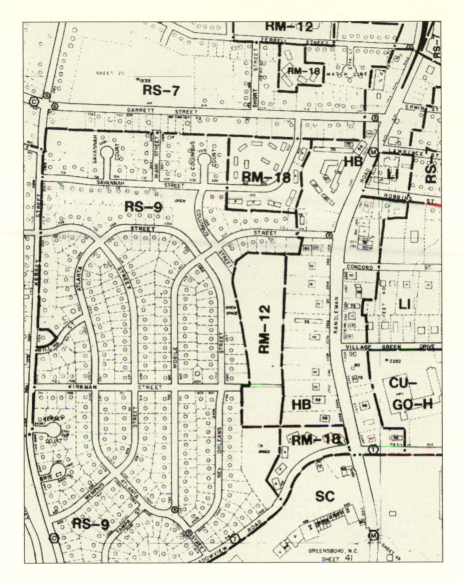

Figure 9. Each zoning ordinance includes a map that places the land subject to zoning in various zoning districts.

As local governments have more finely tuned and limited the permitted uses in each district, the number of different zoning districts has multiplied. For example, instead of a single residential district, a modern zoning ordinance may have five or ten different residential districts—one for single-family residences on large lots, one for single-family residences on small lots, one for multifamily residences, and another for mobile homes. Similarly, a single business district may now be subdivided into separate

Type of District	Uses Allowed
Residential ⟶	Residential
Business ⟶	Business + Residential
Industrial ⟶	Industrial + Business + Residential

Figure 10. Hierarchy of uses in early zoning districts.

zoning districts for *neighborhood business*, *highway commercial*, *central business*, and *shopping center* uses. While a small town or rural county may still only have three or four zoning districts, a typical contemporary city zoning ordinance may now have twenty or thirty different zoning districts.

Zoning districts these days are rarely cumulative. While many zoning ordinances were originally adopted primarily to protect residential property values, modern zoning addresses broader public purposes, such as promoting economic development. A local government may determine that because of utility, highway, and rail access, an area should be reserved exclusively for future industrial development. If an area particularly suited for industrial development were to be developed for residential use, industrial development would have to be located elsewhere, and local government might have to provide new services at considerable expense—if in fact any other suitable sites even existed. Also, if part of the area were first developed for residential uses, its residents might well then want to keep future industry out of their residential neighborhood. To prevent these difficulties and keep the site available for future industrial uses, many cities now no longer permit residential uses in an industrial zoning district.

Another complication added to zoning in the past twenty years has been the increasing use of *overlay zones*. These are special zones in which requirements are imposed in addition to the basic or underlying zoning district requirements. For example, if a river runs through a city, special flood hazard requirements (such as special setback, building elevation, or flood-proofing requirements) may be imposed on all property lying within the flood hazard area adjacent to the river. So a new "floodplain" district is created that contains all of the special flood hazard development standards and that district is applied to all land in the flood hazard area. But the new district does not replace whatever zoning district was already in place; rather, it acts in addition to—or overlays—the basic use districts, whether they be residential, business, or industrial. Development in the overlay district must comply with requirements of both the overlay district and basic district (see Figure 11.) Typical overlay districts include *floodplain districts*, *historic districts*, *airport districts*, and *highway corridor districts*.

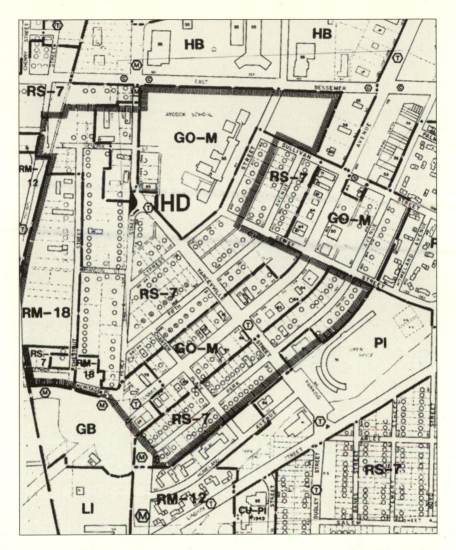

Figure 11. When an overlay district is adopted, the requirements of both the underlying zoning district and the special overlay district apply. In the example pictured above, the land within the bold, cross-hatched line must comply with the zoning ordinance's overlay historic district standards (thus the "HD") as well as meeting the standards for whatever basic zoning district it is in (such as the RM-18, RS-7, or GO-M district).

Zoning districts may also be created that allow only development approved by a *special-* or *conditional-use permit* (see the next section for a discussion of these permits). In North Carolina these *special-use* or *conditional-use districts* can be created only at the landowner's request. These and other specialized districts are often called *floating districts* because they are defined in the text of the zoning ordinance but are not actually applied to the zoning map except upon petition by a landowner.

Modern zoning ordinances and practices have been criticized for being too rigid in their separation of uses, for producing sterile neighborhoods with no commercial uses, and for unduly separating homes from workplaces and shopping. Ironically, one of the principal responses to this criticism has been to create yet another zoning district. Many ordinances now contain a *planned unit development* (PUD) district that allows a large site to be developed with a mixture of land uses according to an approved overall site plan. For example, a large tract may be developed with a mix of single-family and multifamily housing, with part of the site also devoted to commercial and office uses. Another option increasingly being discussed is to add residential districts to accommodate *neotraditional* developments—houses clustered on smaller lots, with some neighborhood-scale commercial and office development and a strong pedestrian focus.

It is important to remember that zoning an area in no way requires a rigid separation of different land uses even though that is the way many ordinances have been structured. Each city and county can custom design its ordinance to include whatever number of districts and use restrictions that seem appropriate in that particular place.

Use Restrictions

Within each zoning district there is a list of *permitted uses*. These are sometimes called *uses by right* because they are automatically allowed in that district. For example, a zoning district might list single-family residences, duplexes, fire and police stations, schools, and temporary construction offices as permitted uses. Other land uses would thus be prohibited.

In the past twenty years many zoning ordinances have added innovative provisions allowing some "maybes" between those uses that are automatically permitted and those that are prohibited in a particular district. The local government may determine that certain uses are suitable for a particular zoning district only if specified conditions are met and only after individual review. For example, it may determine that a multifamily residential development is permissible in a single-family zoning district if the development will be on a site of at least two acres and there is a twenty-foot-wide vegetated buffer maintained between the development and adjacent single family lots. Such uses are allowed only after an individual makes an application for the use and local government approves it and grants a permit for it.

A zoning ordinance calls these uses *conditional uses*, *special uses*, or *special exceptions*, terms that are interchangeable, having the same legal definition. The zoning ordinance itself must set out the conditions under which each conditional use will be allowed. The city or county is not allowed to make a case-by-case discretionary review of each project; the ordinance itself must spell out the standards for obtaining such a permit and a specific list of allowable uses. When someone wants to apply for a conditional-use permit, a town or county board holds a hearing to take evidence on whether the project meets these standards. The governing board, the planning board, or the board of adjustment (or some combination) is responsible for holding a hearing and making the decision. Staff members may not make decisions on special- or conditional-use permits.

For example, a zoning ordinance for a single-family zoning district may allow duplexes as a conditional use, but only on lots of a certain size, with a buffer to screen the property, and only if the developer can show that the project will not have a significant adverse effect on neighboring property values. In order to determine whether these standards have been met, the board must hold a formal hearing to take evidence on the matter and issue a written decision. The burden is on the applicant to produce sufficient evidence to establish that the proposed duplex meets the standards. Once the applicant presents sufficient evidence, the applicant is entitled to a permit unless contradictory evidence is also presented. In such a case the board votes on whether or not the standards are met.

Many zoning ordinances contain a table or schedule of permitted uses that graphically displays how each use is treated in each district. Figure 12 (page 26) illustrates a typical list of permitted uses.

Dimensional Requirements

In addition to specifying which kinds of land uses are permitted in each zoning district, zoning ordinances also have standards for what sizes of lots and buildings are allowed. Standards for lots typically specify minimum lot size and minimum construction setbacks. For example, a particular residential zoning district may require a minimum lot size of 10,000 square feet for each dwelling unit and may require the house to be located at least 50 feet from the front property line, 20 feet from the rear property line, and 10 feet from each side property line. In a different residential district the minimum lot size may be 20,000 square feet, with the same front, rear, and side yard setbacks. The ordinance may also establish minimum lot widths and a minimum street frontage for each lot.

Zoning standards for building dimensions typically set maximum height and structural bulk limits. For example, a neighborhood commercial district may limit building height to no more than 35 feet and building

TABLE 30–4–5–1 PERMITTED USE SCHEDULE

ZONING DISTRICTS

USE TYPES	Ref SIC	AG	RS40	RS30	RS20	RS15	RS12	RS9	RS7	RS5	RM8	RM12	RM18	RM26	LO	OM	OH	NB	LB	GB	HB	CB	CS	CP	CLI	HI	PI	LUC
RECREATIONAL USES (CONTINUED)																												
Public Parks	7990	D	D	D	D	D	D	D	D	D	D	D	D	D	D	D	D	D	D	D	D	D	D	D	D	D	D	1
Public Recreation Facilities	7990	D	D	D	D	D	D	D	D	D	D	D	D	D	D	D	D	D	D	D	D	D	D	D	D	D	S	2
Riding Stables	7999	S	S																								S	2
Shooting Ranges, Indoor	7999	S	S																	S	D	D	D	D	S	D	S	3
Shooting Ranges, Outdoor	7999	S	S																				D					5
Skating Rinks	7999																			P	P	P	P	P		D	P	3
Sports Instructional Schools	7999	S																	P	P	P	P	D	P	P	P	P	3
Sports & Recreation Clubs, Indoor	7997																		P	P	P	P	P	D	P	P	P	3
Swim and Tennis Clubs	7997	S	S	S	S	S	S	S	S	S	S	S	S	S										D			D	3
EDUCATIONAL AND INSTITUTIONAL USES																												
Ambulance Services	4119	P													P	P	P			P	P	P	P	P	P	P	P	3
Auditoriums, Coliseums, or Stadiums	0000	D	D	D	D	D	D	D	D	D	D	D	D	D	P	P	P		P	P	P	P	P	D	D	D	P	3
Cemeteries/Mausoleums	0000	D	D																								S	2
Churches	8661	P	D	D	D	D	D	D	D	D	D	D	D	D	D	D	D	D	D	D	D	D	D	D	D	D	D	3
Colleges or Universities	8220	S																			P	P	P	P	P	S	P	3
Correctional Institutions	9223	S																			P	P	P	P		P	S	4
Day Care Centers, Adult (5 or less, Hom. Occ)	8322	D	D	D	D	D	D	D	D	D	D	D	D	D	D	D	D	D	D	D	D	D	D	D	D	D	D	1
Day Care Centers, Adult (6 or More)	8322	S	S												P	P	P	P	P	P	P	P	P	P	P	P	P	3
Day Care Centers, Child (5 or less, Hom. Occ)	8351	D	D	D	D	D	D	D	D	D	D	D	D	D	D	D	D	D	D	D	D	D	D	D	D	D	D	1
Day Care Centers, Child (6 or more)	8351	S	S												P	P	P	P	P	P	P	P	P	P	P	P	P	3
Elementary or Secondary Schools	8211	D	D	D	D	D	D	D	D	D	D	D	D	D	D	D	D	D	D	D	D	D	D	D	D	D	D	3
Fire Stations	9224	P	P	P	P	P	P	P	P	P	P	P	P	P	P	P	P	P	P	P	P	P	P	P	P	P	P	3
Fraternities or Sororities (Univ. or College)	0000																											3
Government Offices	9000														P	P	P	P	P	P	P	P	P	P	P	P	P	3
Hospitals	8062																				S	S	S				P	3
Libraries	8231														S	S	S	S	S	S	P	P	P	P	P	P	P	3
Museums or Art Galleries	8412	S	P	P											P	P	P	P	P	P	P	P	P	P	P	P	P	3
Nursing and Convalescent Homes	8050	P	P												P	P	P	P	P	P	P	P	P	P	P	P	P	3
Orphanages	8361	S																										3
Police Stations, Neighborhood	9221	P	P												P	P	P	P	P	P	P	P	P	P	P	P	P	3
Post Offices	0000														P	P	P	P	P	P	P	P	P	P	P	P	P	3
Psychiatric Hospitals	8063														P	P	P	P	P	P	P	P	P	P	P	P	P	3
Retreat Centers	0000	S													P	P	P	P	P	P	P	P	P	P	P	P	P	3

P=USE BY RIGHT D= DEVELOPMENT STANDARDS S= SPECIAL USE PERMIT REQUIRED Z=OVERLAY ZONING REQUIRED
*=INDICATES ADDITIONAL DISTRICT REQUIREMENTS SEE SECTION 30-4-5.3

30–4–33

Figure 12. A table of uses, like the one depicted above from the Greensboro, North Carolina, zoning ordinance, sets out whether each particular land use is permitted automatically, permitted under certain conditions, or prohibited in each zoning district (see key at bottom of table).

square footage to 5,000 square feet or less, to cover no more than 50 percent of the lot area.

Other Typical Zoning Requirements

Land use and lot and building size limits provide the basis for a zoning ordinance, but modern zoning increasingly specifies other land development standards as well. Typical provisions these days include standards on landscaping, parking, signs, flood hazards, watershed protection, and historic preservation.

Landscaping and parking requirements typically apply to nonresidential land uses. For example, new businesses and industries may be required to have a planted buffer to provide a separation between uses or to assist in protecting water quality. Zoning ordinances may require provision of landscaping along the street front or in parking areas to enhance the community's appearance. The size of the area to be landscaped and even the type of plants may be specified. In order to prevent street congestion or impositions on neighbors, ordinances usually require a new business to provide a minimum amount of off-street parking on site. For example, a restaurant may be required to provide one parking place for each four seats provided its clients, an office building may be required to provide one parking place for each 250 square feet of floor space in the building, and an industry may be required to provide two parking places for every three employees. The zoning ordinance will usually also specify the size of the parking places, whether they must be paved, and where on the site they can be located.

Zoning ordinances often include sign regulations, though sometimes a separate sign ordinance covers these regulations. Typical sign regulations include limits on location (for example, no billboards allowed in residential zoning districts and a minimum distance between billboards); size (maximum height and square footage); and types (for example, a prohibition on flashing lights, portable signs, or windblown signs). Regulation of signs raises some constitutional issues related to free speech that are discussed further in Chapter 9.

Many zoning ordinances include standards to reduce flood hazards and to protect public water supplies. A jurisdiction must regulate flood hazards in order for property owners to qualify for federal flood insurance. Typical standards include prohibition of structures or fill dirt in the floodway, elevation of structures above flood levels, and the safe location of electrical and plumbing systems. The state of North Carolina requires all local governments that have jurisdiction over land that drains into a public surface water supply to regulate development so as to minimize contamination of these lakes and rivers. Such regulations limit the number of residential units per acre, limit the amount of built-on area in commercial or industrial areas, require vegetated buffers along the shoreline, and limit the placement of hazardous materials in these critical areas.

Historic preservation efforts have engendered another kind of zoning regulation. Many local governments have placed older neighborhoods into *historic district overlay zones* to preserve the special character of these communities. The zoning restrictions may limit the alteration of the exteriors of these structures to those improvements that are compatible with the historic character of the neighborhood. The ordinances typically require that a historic preservation commission issue a *certificate of appropriateness* before new buildings can be constructed or existing structures altered. These regulations may also require a mandatory waiting period of up to a year before a structure in a historic district can be demolished.

4 Overview of the Zoning Process

A number of different local government bodies participate in the zoning process. The city council or county board of commissioners, the planning board, and the zoning board of adjustment all play key roles. In addition, local government planning and zoning staff provide essential support in zoning administration and enforcement. The kind of zoning decision being considered determines which groups get involved. This chapter provides a brief overview of the types of zoning decisions and the governmental bodies who make them. The following chapters then discuss the types of zoning decisions in more detail.

Types of Zoning Decisions

Zoning decisions can be grouped into four categories: *legislative*, *quasi-judicial*, *advisory*, and *administrative*. Who makes these decisions, and even more importantly, what rules on the process must be followed in making them vary significantly among these categories. Governing boards usually make legislative decisions but can also make quasi-judicial decisions. Planning boards usually make advisory decisions but can also make quasi-judicial decisions. Knowing the type of decision is vital to determining what decision-making process should be used.

Legislative zoning decisions affect the entire community by setting general policies applicable through the zoning ordinance. They include decisions to adopt, amend, or repeal the zoning ordinance (including the zoning map). Because legislative zoning decisions have such an important impact on landowners, neighbors, and the public, state law mandates broad public notice and hearing requirements for these decisions. Broad public discussion and careful deliberation are encouraged and substantial discretion on these decisions is allowed. These are called *legislative* decisions because they are generally made by the local government body, which "legislates" or sets policy. This body is either the city council or county board of commissioners. The state legislature does not make or review these decisions.

Quasi-judicial decisions involve the application of zoning policies to individual situations. Examples include variances, special- and conditional-use permits (even if issued by the governing board), appeals, and interpretations. These decisions involve two key elements—the finding of facts regarding the specific proposal and the exercise of some limited discretion in applying predetermined policies to the situation. Since quasi-judicial decisions do not involve setting new policies, the broad public notice requirements that exist for legislative zoning decisions do not apply. However, the courts have imposed fairly strict procedural requirements on these decisions in order to protect the legal rights of the parties involved. Quasi-judicial decisions are most often assigned to boards of adjustment, appointed by the governing board. But these decisions can also be assigned to the planning board or to the governing board itself.

Advisory decisions are made by bodies that may recommend decisions on a matter but have no final decision-making authority over it. The most common example is the advice on rezoning petitions given by county planning boards to boards of county commissioners. Advisory review is sometimes mandated by the state in order to secure additional public review of proposed zoning policy choices. There are no special rules set by state law or by the courts on how advisory zoning decisions are made, so there is little further discussion of advisory decisions in this book. Such decisions can, however, provide thoughtful review and commentary on proposed zoning policies. The absence of further discussion about them here reflects more the lack of special rules or restrictions placed on them than any lack of importance of advisory comments.

Administrative decisions are typically made by professional staff in various government departments. Such decisions cover the day-to-day nondiscretionary matters related to the implementation of a zoning ordinance, including issuing basic permits, interpreting the zoning ordinance, and enforcing it.

Zoning Hearings

Before a zoning decision is made, it is often useful and sometimes necessary to solicit information and public comment. State law requires that a formal hearing be conducted prior to making legislative and quasi-judicial zoning decisions. No hearings are required for advisory or administrative zoning decisions. Since the forums for soliciting information for both legislative and quasi-judicial zoning decisions are typically called "zoning hearings," many people mistakenly believe that hearings for the two kinds of decisions are conducted the same way. This is not the case, though citizens and board members accustomed to one type of hearing may well not realize they have to follow an entirely different set of ground rules when attending a hearing on a different type of zoning decision. Careful attention to the type of zoning decision involved is necessary to prevent use of the wrong set of procedures.

Legislative hearings are used in making legislative zoning decisions to gather opinions on a proposed policy. They are formal mechanisms to secure citizens' comments on a specific proposal. These are often called *public hearings*. They must be conducted in a fair, orderly manner to allow citizen opinion to be expressed directly to those making zoning policy decisions. Public hearings are run by the governing board, with both newspaper and individual mailed notice. Speakers are not placed under oath and the board need not make findings at the conclusion of the hearing. Reasonable time limits can be placed on speakers and on the overall length of the hearing.

Evidentiary hearings are used in making quasi-judicial decisions. They provide a more formal means of gathering evidence before a decision is made in the application of a zoning ordinance to an individual situation. Such decisions include variances, special- and conditional-use permits, and appeals of the zoning officer's interpretations. The purpose of an evidentiary hearing is to gather facts, not to solicit citizen opinions. These hearings are much like a court proceeding—witnesses present testimony, exhibits are submitted, detailed minutes are kept, and a formal written decision is rendered by the body running the hearing.

Figure 13 (page 32) summarizes some of the key differences between legislative public hearings and evidentiary hearings.

In addition to these two types of formal hearings, many local governments often also conduct more informal *public meetings* to inform the public about a pending matter and solicit comments. Such forums are most often used for advisory zoning decisions or as a prelude to a legislative hearing. They are not mandated by state law, and they may be conducted in any manner the city or county deems appropriate.

Zoning Boards, Staff, and Other Parties in the Zoning Process

North Carolina law gives a local government considerable flexibility in determining how to allocate zoning decisions to various boards and agencies; the three boards described below commonly take charge of major aspects of zoning. Smaller towns often combine several of these boards into a single board. In addition to these boards, staff and others may be involved.

Governing board. The local governing board controlling local zoning comprises a city council or county board of commissioners. This governing board makes final policy decisions on zoning. It adopts and amends the ordinance and appoints the members of the other citizen boards involved. The governing board is responsible for adopting a zoning system that fits the needs of the individual community. Therefore the governing

	Legislative	Evidentiary
Type of Zoning Decision	Legislative (adoptive, rezonings).	Quasi-judicial (variances, special- and conditional-use permits, appeals only).
Notice of Hearing	Newspaper and mailed notice.	Notice to parties only.
Speakers at Hearing	Anyone. Reasonable limits on time and number of speakers.	Witnesses.
Evidence	None.	Substantial, competent, nonrepetitious material evidence.
Contact Outside the Hearing	Permitted.	No outside discussions or fact finding allowed.
Findings	None.	Written findings of fact required.
Records	Regular minutes.	Detailed record of testimony.

Figure 13. Key differences between legislative and evidentiary zoning hearings.

board must first understand and approve the policies that serve as the foundation for zoning and then conduct ongoing reviews of the zoning system to ensure it is working as intended.

Planning board. The planning board or planning commission is a group of citizens who provide advice to the governing board on zoning issues. The planning board can be of any size (it must have at least three members) and may be constituted however the governing board deems appropriate. The governing board must appoint a planning board before adopting a zoning ordinance.

Counties must refer all zoning amendments to the planning board for review. Most cities also refer zoning amendments to their planning boards, although state law does not require it. Some governing boards assign to their planning boards either advisory or final decision-making authority for special- and conditional-use permits. Planning boards may help with a number of nonzoning matters, such as development of a comprehensive plan, community and economic development programs, and the like. The governing board may also assign to the planning board any or all of the functions of a board of adjustment (see below).

Board of adjustment. The board of adjustment is rarely involved in setting zoning policies. This board interprets and applies the standards that have been placed in the zoning ordinance by the governing board. The governing board appoints at least five members to this board, each with a set, three-year term. The board of adjustment hears individual quasi-judicial cases, such as appeals, requests for special- or conditional-use permits, and variance petitions. The statutes generally require a four-fifths vote to approve a permit or variance or overrule the staff on an interpretation of the ordinance. Decisions of this board may be appealed directly to the courts.

Staff. City or county managers hire the staff members that support the zoning function. Staff in the planning department, inspections department, and manager's office provide support to the zoning process, preparing drafts of the ordinances, processing permits, enforcing the ordinance, and keeping the records of the citizen boards. In a few instances in North Carolina, the planning staff is hired directly by the planning board. Local governments can also secure staff assistance in zoning from private consultants, from the state Division of Community Assistance, or from regional councils of government.

Others. There are a number of other entities that may play some role in zoning. A historic preservation commission, for example, may review permits related to specially designated historic districts or landmarks. Locally appointed community appearance commissions and economic development commissions rarely work directly in zoning implementation, but should closely coordinate their work with the zoning program.

Figure 14 (page 34) illustrates a typical allocation of zoning responsibilities among these groups.

Public Access to Meetings and Records

In North Carolina, as in many states, the law requires most public meetings and records to be open to the public.

Meetings. Whenever a majority of the members of any public board (and any committee of a board) meet to discuss business, advance notice of the meeting must be provided, full and accurate minutes of the meeting must be kept, and the public must be allowed to observe the meeting. There are some very limited instances where a board is allowed to conduct closed sessions, such as when the board is getting advice from its attorney on a pending lawsuit or when the board is conducting a personnel evaluation of one of its staff members. It is rare that a zoning matter will qualify for discussion in a closed session. Open public meetings are

Agency	Primary role	Other roles
Governing Board (city council, board of county commissioners)	Legislative decisions: adopts ordinances, amendments, policy statements, budgets; approves acquisitions; makes appointments to other bodies.	May also serve as planning agency; may approve plats and special-use permits.
Planning Agency (planning board, planning commission, planning committee of governing board)	Advisory decisions: sponsors planning studies; recommends policies, coordinates public participation; must recommend initial zoning ordinance.	May also serve as board of adjustment; approve or review plats.
Board of Adjustment	Quasi-judicial decisions: hearing zoning appeals and applications for variances, special-use permits.	
Staff (planning department, inspections department, community development department, clerk)	Administrative decisions: issue permits, conduct technical studies, initiate enforcement; advise manager.	

Figure 14. Typical roles of zoning agencies.

required for everything from a planning board workshop on a rezoning proposal to a board of adjustment hearing on a variance petition. The governing board could meet in closed session, however, to hear a report on the progress of a suit resulting from a zoning decision or to conduct a personnel review regarding the zoning administrator.

Records. All documents, reports, and letters sent or received in the course of business are considered public records, including staff reports presented to the citizen boards, minutes of meetings, and staff logs of complaints received. These records must be made available for public inspection at reasonable times in the offices where the records are normally kept. A reasonable fee can be charged for copying these materials.

5 Legislative Decisions: Adoption, Rezonings, and Text Amendments

In North Carolina, most cities and many counties already have a zoning ordinance in place. As communities grow and change, however, they often find their zoning ordinance does not adequately address new issues or new development proposals. Thus many local governments are faced with the prospect of amending their zoning ordinance. This most often occurs when a landowner asks for a change in zoning to accommodate a new development proposal. Sometimes a zoning change is proposed by an elected official, the planning board, or the staff. Or a neighborhood group or other interested citizens may propose a change. Though many zoning ordinances purport to limit requests for changes to those from a landowner or a local government body, such limitations are of dubious legality. In some cases, the city or county may have acquired new territory that has to be zoned. The special rules discussed in this chapter apply to all such legislative zoning decisions, from the initial adoption of a zoning ordinance to its amendment or entire repeal. But since more than 400 existing zoning ordinances have already been adopted in the state, and since total repeal is almost unheard of, most of the discussion in this chapter focuses on zoning amendments.

When local governing boards adopt or change a zoning ordinance, they should expect scrutiny—even controversy. Packed public hearings, numerous phone calls, letters, visits, and high emotions will be standard fare. Such public response is understandable—a rezoning can affect many properties and lives. Local governing boards would be wise to carefully consider the policy and legal aspects of zoning changes as they propose changes in the ordinance.

The staff, planning board, and governing board must carefully evaluate the policy implications of a proposed zoning change. Is the change consistent with the adopted plan for the area? What impact will it have on public services such as roads, schools, police, fire, water, and sewer? What impact will it have on the property owners and the neighbors? What policy precedent does it set for future requests for amendments? These and other considerations need to be carefully discussed and considered before amending a zoning ordinance.

Because zoning changes can have dramatic effects on many people, the legislature requires special procedures to be followed whenever a zoning ordinance is adopted, amended, or repealed. The procedures ensure that those most directly affected by zoning ordinances—the landowners and immediate neighbors—have notice of the proposed decision and a full opportunity to make their views known. They also ensure that the local government follows a careful, deliberate decision-making process.

Several kinds of special requirements for zoning amendments are discussed in this chapter. They include requirements on giving notice of the proposed legislative zoning decision to affected persons; on holding public hearings; on requiring rezonings to be approved by a special majority vote if a valid protest petition has been filed; on the relationship of zoning changes and the comprehensive plan; and on limiting small-scale rezonings. These kinds of requirements are contained in state law and apply to all zoning ordinances, unless the General Assembly makes a special amendment in state law at the request of a particular city or county. Individual zoning ordinances may contain other requirements, added at the discretion of the local governing board. Typical additional locally imposed requirements include a requirement to post notice of proposed rezonings at the site and a requirement for a minimum waiting period between consideration of rezoning petitions for the same site. If these additional requirements are included in a zoning ordinance, they are binding and must be followed.

Notice of Proposed Amendments

There are several ways citizens can be notified of a proposed rezoning or zoning amendment. While a local government can always use as many notification tools as it desires, state law establishes two minimum steps.

Requirement 1. There must be at least two newspaper advertisements of the public hearing on all zoning amendments. This applies both to amendments to the text of the zoning ordinance and to rezonings (amendments of the zoning map). The advertisements must be run in a newspaper of general circulation in the area affected. Publication in a property owners' newsletter or a free advertising paper is allowed, but these will not count as the required published notice. Ads may be published in fine print in the legal ads section of the newspaper, though some cities and counties use larger (and more expensive) display advertisements. The first notice must be published at least ten days before the hearing, but not more than twenty-five days before the hearing. The second notice must appear in a separate calendar week.

Requirement 2. Starting in 1985, property owners most directly affected by a zoning map amendment—a rezoning—must get individual mailed notice of the hearing. This notice goes to the owners of all abutting property as well as property to be rezoned. The county tax records determine who the owners of the property are. An updated title search to determine whether the property has changed hands since the tax listing is not required. This notice may be sent by first-class mail (it does not have to be sent by registered or certified mail). A city or county can require someone proposing a rezoning to compile the list of owners who get this mailed notice, although the staff usually does the actual mailing. Where large-scale rezonings are involved—those affecting more than fifty parcels with at least fifty different landowners—cities and counties have the option of using an expanded published notice instead of individual mailed notices. With this alternative, the local government must run four half-page newspaper ads for the hearing (each ad appearing in a separate week), post a notice of the hearing on the site, and mail letters to those property owners who live outside the newspaper's area of circulation.

An individual zoning ordinance can establish notice requirements in addition to these two required by state law. Any such additional requirements are binding and must be observed. The most common additional requirement is placement of a sign on the site notifying the public of a proposed rezoning.

If the notice requirements above are not strictly followed, any action local government takes to rezone will be invalidated by the courts if the rezoning is challenged in court.

Hearings

Local government can use a variety of forums to gather public comment on proposed zoning changes. Informal neighborhood meetings, meetings with interested groups, planning board hearings, and formal public hearings by the governing board are all frequently used to solicit comments. Most such meetings are optional and it is up to each local government to decide which kind is appropriate. State law does require the governing board to hold formal public hearings before adopting, amending, or repealing zoning. (Special legislation allows planning boards to run such hearings in a few North Carolina communities.) Not every zoning amendment petition goes to public notice and hearing, however. Some local governments allow the planning board to screen out some petitions. But in order for the petition ultimately to be adopted, it must have gone through these public notice and hearing requirements.

A formal legislative public hearing on zoning changes is a chance for citizens to make their views known directly to the governing board. Because a legislative public hearing is not an evidentiary hearing, there is no need to have sworn testimony. (Evidentiary hearings are required for variances and special- and conditional-use permits and are discussed in Chapter 6). Persons appearing at public hearings are not limited to legally relevant topics. Citizens are free to offer opinions in the hearing and even to lobby board members before and after the hearing. The board need not make any formal findings at the conclusion of the hearing or explain its decision. The motives of the board in making a decision are generally irrelevant unless a clearly impermissible motive such as racial discrimination is present. But such legislative hearings do need to be conducted in a fair and impartial manner. An overall time limit can be set for the hearing, and reasonable time limits can be imposed on individual speakers. The governing board is not obligated to allow everyone present to speak, but if limits on the number of speakers are imposed they must be fair. For example, the board may arrange for an equal number of proponents and opponents to speak.

Must an additional hearing be held if the governing board decides to make changes in the proposed action after the public hearing? It depends on how substantial the change is. For example, if notice is given and a hearing is held on a proposal to rezone a parcel from a low-density residential district to a high-density residential zoning district, is another hearing required if the city council decides to rezone the parcel to a medium-density residential district after hearing comments at the public hearing?

If the action taken is not substantially different from that originally proposed, no additional hearings are required. A change to a zoning proposal is not considered "substantially different" if the change is favorable to those who requested that change, if the action taken is the same fundamental character as that proposed in the original public notice, and if the notice indicated that changes might be made after hearing public comments. As a general rule, amending the proposal to rezone less land or to allow a similar but less significant change in its uses will not require a new hearing.

Protest Petitions

Neither the landowner nor the neighbors have any legal right to the continuation of any particular zoning on a piece of property. A decision on whether and how to rezone property is left to the discretion and good judgment of elected officials, the notion being that if the citizens do not approve of their decisions, the remedy is at the ballot box. But in cities a further protection, the *protest petition*, provides a small degree of additional stability to zoning, allowing citizens to have more say in a decision. The protest petition option was included in the original 1916 New York zoning ordinance and the model code that was adopted by most states, North Carolina included. The state statutes provide that if the owners of a sufficient amount of land most directly affected file such a petition, a municipal zoning amendment can be adopted only if approved by a three-fourths majority of the city council. Landowners of 20 percent of a *qualifying area* must file the petition with the city before the public hearing on the proposed zoning change in order to trigger this special voting requirement. This protest option must be provided by city governments, but the state statutes do not require counties to allow protest petitions for zoning changes. Several North Carolina counties have voluntarily included such provisions in their zoning ordinances.

While the statute is not entirely clear on this subject, a *qualifying area* appears to include any one of the following: (1) the property being rezoned; (2) a strip of land 100 feet wide in the rear of the property; (3) a strip of land 100 feet wide across the street from the property being rezoned; (4) a strip of land 100 feet wide on one side of the property; and (5) a strip of land with 100-feet-wide strips on the other side of the property. These areas are illustrated in Figure 15 (page 40). The difficulty in interpretation arises when the area being rezoned has an irregular shape or multiple street frontages. While cities may resolve this question different ways, most categorize the surrounding property as front, rear, or one of two sides, and let the 100-foot requirement apply to any one of those four areas. The 20 percent requirement refers to the land area, not the number of owners. For example, if a single person owns 20 percent of the land in one of the qualifying areas—say, the rear of the property being zoned—that individual can file a protest petition and trigger the three-fourths vote requirement. Finally, the 100-foot strip for a qualifying area is measured from the boundary of the area being rezoned, not from the property line. Figure 16 (page 41) illustrates how a buffer can be used to prevent an adjacent property owner from having the right to file a protest petition.

Certain procedural requirements must be met for the protest petition to be valid. The petition must be in writing; it must be signed by the owners of the property; and it must be filed at least two working days before the advertised public hearing. Some cities may require the protest to be filed on a form they provide.

Protest petitions can be used only to object to changes in zoning. They may not be filed to protest the initial zoning of an area, such as when zoning is first adopted for newly annexed territory of a city. They likewise cannot be used to protest modest changes in special- and conditional-use district zoning amendments. (See page 54 for a discussion of special- and conditional-use districts.)

Waiting Periods

Rezoning an area involves substantial work for a number of parties. The owner usually prepares an application; the city or county staff must undertake a technical review of the proposal; the planning board and

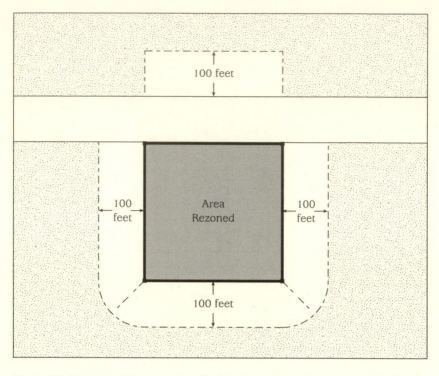

Figure 15. Protest petitions may be filed by landowners being rezoned or by the owners of any one of the four sides shown above.

governing board must carefully consider and rule on the proposal; neighbors must monitor the proposal and attend hearings to present their concerns; and members of the public must present their concerns about the future development of their community.

Because rezoning involves so much time, effort, and money, once a rezoning proposal is rejected, some local zoning ordinances require a waiting period before any new rezoning proposal for that land can be considered. This helps prevent the waste of public and private resources spent on repetitious reviews of the same project. A local zoning ordinance may provide that if a rezoning proposal is denied, no other rezonings will be considered for that property for a period of six months to two years.

Such provisions are binding and must be observed. The state does not require a waiting period, so unless the local zoning ordinance provides one, an owner can come back to the city council or county board of commissioners as often as he or she wishes.

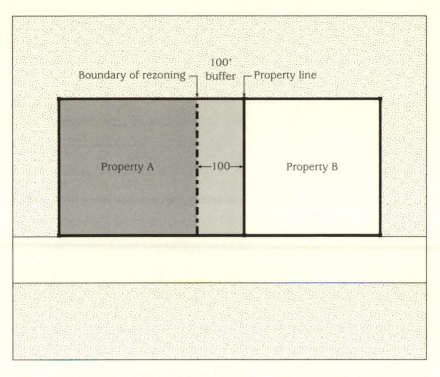

Figure 16. If a 100-foot buffer is left between the area being rezoned (a portion of Property A) and Owner B's property line, Owner B has no right to file a protest petition.

Zoning and the Comprehensive Plan

Most local governments that have a zoning ordinance also have a comprehensive plan or a land-use plan. The relationship between the plan and the zoning ordinance can be a powerful factor in land-use regulation. The relationship between plans and regulations in North Carolina, however, is not as strong as in some states.

Several states require local governments to prepare land-use plans. In those states there are usually requirements as to what the plan must include and how it is to be prepared, and the relationship of plan to regulation is specified. The only mandate for local land-use plans in North Carolina is the requirement of the Coastal Area Management Act, which requires that plans be prepared in the twenty coastal counties. Yet even in the coastal area there is no requirement that there be zoning and only a very limited requirement for consistency between the plans and any zoning that is enacted. So there are few legal mandates regarding land-use planning in this state.

State zoning statutes do provide that all zoning must be "in accordance with a comprehensive plan." The North Carolina courts have not, however, read this to mean that all zoning decisions must be precisely measured against a separately adopted land-use plan. Rather, the courts have ruled that zoning decisions must be based on a reasoned consideration of land-use issues facing the entire community, which means that competent technical studies must serve as the foundation of zoning decisions and that such studies and plans and public input must be thoroughly considered as zoning decisions are made. A zoning amendment that is clearly contrary to the policies in an adopted city or county plan, particularly if the rezoning involves only a small area of land, is suspect and may well be invalidated by the courts unless a clear public purpose for the amendment has been established.

Despite the fact that land-use plans are not required in many areas, a fairly consistent pattern of local land-use planning has emerged in North Carolina. Many cities and counties have undertaken planning efforts to help guide their community's future. These efforts usually involve substantial data collection and technical analysis, public discussion of goals and objectives, and attempts to reach consensus on what the community should be like in the future and how that will be achieved. The planning process involves examination of changes in population and development and the consideration of the need for and ability to provide necessary public services like water, sewer, schools, parks, roads, police, fire, and emergency services. It also involves consideration of the preservation and enhancement of important community attributes such as a clean and healthy environment, good quality jobs and housing, vibrant commercial areas, historic structures and community aesthetics, and the like. The purpose of these planning efforts is the establishment of clear, consistent, predictable, coordinated community policies that will serve as the long-term foundation for day-to-day public investment and regulatory decisions.

If a community does adopt a land-use plan, there is no legal requirement that all zoning decisions exactly match up to it. The plan is just that—a plan or guide and not a regulation. But the plan, and all of the studies and discussion that led to it, does provide the general policy foundation for zoning decisions. The law, as well as good planning practice and common sense, suggests that those policies be carefully considered as each zoning decision is made.

Spot Zoning

Zoning is an exercise of governmental power for the overall public good. The courts will generally defer to the judgment of elected officials as to just what this overall public good is. But when the zoning power is applied to a small area in a way that is different from how it applies to the surrounding area, the overall public good may not be served. If such a zoning action, called *spot zoning*, is challenged in court, the court will not presume the zoning to be valid, but rather will very carefully review the zoning to ensure that it is reasonable and in the public interest.

Courts may apply this particular scrutiny to challenges of either the initial zoning of a parcel or rezoning decisions. Just how small the area has to be to raise the spot zoning issue depends on the setting. In the center of a city with many zoning districts, a five-acre rezoning may represent a relatively large zoning district and not be considered spot zoning. On the other hand, in a rural area where thousands of surrounding acres are zoned one way, a five-acre rezoning will be spot zoning. In North Carolina the courts have invalidated spot zonings as small as one lot and as large as seventeen acres.

In some states spot zoning is automatically illegal; not so in North Carolina. Spot zoning is permissible in North Carolina *if* it is *reasonable*. The courts have set out the following four factors to be used in a case-by-case analysis to determine if a particular spot zoning is reasonable:

1. *The size of the tract.* The larger the area of spot zoning the more likely it is to be reasonable. Singling out an individual lot for special zoning treatment is more suspect than creating a zoning district that involves multiple parcels and owners.
2. *Compatibility with an existing comprehensive plan.* If a clear public policy rationale for the different zoning treatment is set out in the local government's comprehensive plan, that evidences a public purpose for the zoning. By contrast, a zoning action that is inconsistent with the plan may indicate special treatment that is contrary to the public interest and thus be unreasonable. Special site characteristics, such as topography, availability of utilities, or access to rail or highways, can also be important in this analysis.
3. *The impact of the zoning decision on the landowner, the immediate neighbors, and the surrounding community.* An action that is of great benefit to the owner and only a mild inconvenience for the neighbors may be reasonable, while a zoning decision that significantly harms the neighbors would be unreasonable.
4. *The relationship between the newly allowed uses in a spot rezoning and the previously allowed uses.* The greater the difference in allowed uses, the more likely the rezoning will be found unreasonable. For example, in an area previously zoned for residential uses, allowing slightly higher residential density may be reasonable while allowing industrial uses would be unreasonable.

Thus, the key question in a court's review of an action challenged as illegal spot zoning is whether the zoning power is being exercised in the public interest rather than for the benefit of a few owners at the expense of the community. Sometimes very small zoning districts are justified and reasonable. However, if they are going to be used, it is up to the local government to do a careful analysis of the above factors, and to place that analysis in the public record, in order to document the reasonableness of the decision.

Contract Zoning and Conditional-Use District Zoning

Contract zoning and similar agreements are illegal in North Carolina. In contract zoning, the government and a landowner enter into a private agreement as to how the zoning power will be exercised. The zoning power must be exercised for the public good, not used as a bargaining chip in ad hoc negotiations with individual land owners. For example, if a local government rezones a property from a residential to a commercial zoning district in return for the owner's promise to build a new swimming pool for the city's park system, this is illegal contract zoning.

Serious disputes between neighbors about adjacent land uses frequently end up as zoning battles. Not only do such battles resolve individual disputes, they often shape the law on how zoning tools must be applied by all cities and counties. A Guilford County dispute between a homeowner seeking peace and quiet and a business owner who needed to expand illustrate this.

Bruce Clapp owned and ran a small operation for drying grain in rural Guilford County, a business begun in 1948. In 1969 he sold a portion of his property to Mr. and Mrs. William Chrismon for a residence. In 1980 Clapp expanded his grain drying operation to a portion of the property immediately behind the Chrismons' house and expanded the business (see Figure 17) to include sale of farm chemicals. The Chrismons were not happy about this and complained to the county. It turned out the entire site was zoned for agricultural and residential uses, so the county told Clapp he could not expand the business. Now Clapp was unhappy. So he promptly asked that the five acres needed for the business expansion be rezoned to allow his business. The county commissioners sided with Clapp and rezoned the property to a district that allowed the operation if he got a conditional-use permit—and they concurrently issued a conditional-use permit. The county was then sued by the Chrismons, who alleged that this was illegal spot zoning and illegal contract zoning.

Figure 17. This is the grain-drying and agricultural business that was built adjacent to the Chrismons' house.

In a key zoning case, the North Carolina Supreme Court upheld the county action. The court said this was indeed spot zoning, but it was not illegal because it was reasonable in this situation. The court found that this business was compatible with and beneficial to the surrounding farm community and that this was not a substantial departure from the uses already present in the neighborhood. The court also allowed the practice of creating a zoning district with only conditional uses (and no automatically approved permitted uses) and allowed the county commissioners to decide on the conditional-use permit at the same time that the rezoning decision was made. This tool, *conditional-use district zoning*, has subsequently been adopted by many North Carolina cities and counties as a way of avoiding illegal contract zoning.

Though not technically contract zoning, the following kind of agreement is also illegal in North Carolina: a landowner requests a rezoning to accommodate a specific project and the city or county governing board considers only that project rather than the full range of uses that would be allowed in the new zoning district. If an owner promises the governing board that the new zoning would be used only for a particular project, that promise is not binding. Once the property is rezoned, the owner (and anyone the person may sell the property to) can undertake any use permitted in the new zoning district. This cannot be corrected by the government attempting to impose a condition or special limitation on the individual rezoning.

Special conditions on a rezoning—such as limiting the site's use to that of the project described by the owner at the hearing or requiring a buffer strip of a certain size—are not enforceable. Only those standards that apply to all property in the zoning district are legally enforceable. If it is clear that the governing board did not consider the full range of uses allowed in the new zoning district, the courts will invalidate the rezoning. For these reasons, many local governments forbid someone proposing a rezoning from even mentioning what specific use is planned for the site. If a specific use is mentioned, the record must clearly show that the governing board was aware of the full range of uses that would be allowed in the new district and that the governing board concluded that any of those permitted uses (not just the specific project proposed) would be suitable.

Conditional-use district zoning is a zoning tool that is increasingly used in North Carolina to avoid these legal problems with contract zoning. This tool allows the local government to legally discuss a particular project with an owner and the neighbors before rezoning a property, but only if the proper procedures are precisely followed. First the owner asks for a rezoning to a new zoning district that does not have any automatically permitted uses, only uses allowed by the issuance of a special- or conditional-use permit. The owner simultaneously applies for a special- or conditional-use permit for a particular project. The rezoning and the permit are processed at the same time, but the governing board treats the two proposals as legally independent, separate decisions. All of the detailed conditions and specific restrictions on the project are then attached to the conditional- or special-use permit (which is legal) rather than to the rezoning itself (which would not be enforceable). This is a complicated process, but it allows zoning to be more carefully tailored to a particular situation. Conditional-use district zoning is legal in North Carolina if it is correctly applied. Conditional-use districts are not exempt, however, from a spot-zoning challenge. If the new district is relatively small—and most of these are—the prudent local government will assure that all of the factors defining reasonable spot zoning are fully considered and that the public hearing record reflects that.

Judicial Review

In North Carolina, the adoption, amendment, and repeal of zoning ordinances can be challenged in court by persons who have a specific personal interest in the decision and whose legal interests are directly and adversely affected by the decision. State statutes provide that a challenge to a zoning ordinance decision must be filed within nine months of the date of the decision. Once the challenge is filed, the court will examine the decision to see if the governing board followed proper procedures. If, for example, there was inadequate public notice of the hearing, the court will void the action taken by the governing board and the zoning will revert to whatever it was before that decision. As a general rule, the courts give legislative zoning decisions the presumption of validity—the court will not second-guess the policy decisions of elected officials. Only those decisions that are clearly unreasonable or abusive of discretion and those that were made using improper procedures will be set aside. The exception to this general rule of judicial deference to the judgment of governing boards comes in court review of spot zoning. There, the local government has the burden of showing that its zoning is reasonable.

6   Quasi-Judicial Decisions

Once the zoning ordinance is adopted or amended, its provisions must be implemented. Citizen requests for variances, special- and conditional-use permits, and appeals of administrative decisions made by the zoning administrator require special handling. Decisions on such issues involve the finding of facts and the exercise of some degree of discretion. They are called *quasi-judicial decisions*, and they are subject to procedural rules set forth by the courts, including the requirement of a formal evidentiary hearing. Quasi-judicial decisions are usually made by the board of adjustment, but they are sometimes handled by the planning boards or the governing board. No matter which citizen board makes such decisions, however, the procedures described in this chapter must be used.

Quasi-judicial zoning decisions differ from legislative zoning decisions in that they do not involve setting new policies. Rather, in quasi-judicial decisions the citizen board acts more like a court applying the ordinance to a specific case. Instead of detailing standards for public notice and hearing, the procedural requirements for quasi-judicial decisions focus on securing a fair and impartial hearing on the merits of the individual cases. The differences in legal requirements for the two different procedures often confuse citizen board members as well as citizens participating in the hearing. In legislative zoning hearings citizens can appear and say whatever is on their mind; community opinions and attitudes are important, legitimate considerations. In evidentiary hearings for quasi-judicial zoning decisions, however, the goal is strictly to gather legally acceptable evidence. Citizen boards should keep this difference clearly in mind, and should fully explain the difference to those appearing at these hearings. A handout for the applicants and neighbors can explain the ground rules for evidentiary hearings and help avoid misunderstandings and legal errors in how these hearings are conducted.

Special Rules for Decision-Making Process

Most quasi-judicial zoning decisions are made by boards of adjustment. However, North Carolina law also allows these decisions to be made by the planning board or the governing board. They must not, however, be assigned to a single staff member. The rules discussed here apply whenever a quasi-judicial zoning decision is involved, regardless of which citizen board makes the decision.

Before making a quasi-judicial decision, the citizen board involved must conduct a fair evidentiary hearing to gather the necessary evidence on which to base a decision. The purpose of this hearing is to gather evidence in order to establish sufficient facts to apply the ordinance. *The purpose is not to gather public opinion about the desirability of the project involved.* Therefore, the broad public notice requirements of legislative decisions (newspaper and mailed notice) do not apply to these hearings. There is no specific statute setting out notice requirements, but it is reasonable to send first-class mailed notice to the parties. Many cities and counties also have established a practice of sending a courtesy mailing about the hearing to the immediate neighbors, and many publish notice in the newspaper or post a notice on the site.

The hearing must be conducted in a fair and impartial manner. While the formal rules of evidence that apply in court need not be rigorously followed, zoning evidentiary hearings are serious proceedings that significantly affect the legal rights of the parties. The following guidelines apply.

Swearing in. Those offering testimony are usually put under oath. This reminds witnesses of the seriousness of the matter and the necessity of presenting factual information, not opinions or speculation. While oaths may be waived if all of the parties agree, many local governments now routinely swear in all witnesses, including the staff members and attorneys who are making presentations.

False testimony. A person who deliberately gives false testimony under oath in a zoning hearing is subject to criminal charges.

Cross-examination. Parties have the right to cross-examine witnesses and to present exhibits.

Time limits. While unduly repetitious or irrelevant testimony can be barred, an arbitrary time limit on the hearing cannot be used.

Hearsay. Hearsay evidence and opinion evidence (unless offered by a properly qualified expert witness) is generally not allowable.

Subpoenas. City boards conducting these hearings have the authority to issue subpoenas to compel testimony or production of evidence deemed necessary to determine the matter. County boards do not have explicit statutory authority to issue subpoenas.

Limits on board members. Members of the decision-making body are not allowed to discuss pending cases outside of the hearing. Only facts presented to the full board at the hearing may be considered. It is permissible for board members to view the site in question before the hearing, but they should not talk about the case with the applicant, neighbors, or staff outside of the hearing. If a member has special knowledge about a site or case, the member should disclose that at the hearing. These rules are designed to ensure that everyone knows all of the facts being considered by the board.

Conflict of interest. If an individual board member has a strong personal interest in a case, he or she must not participate in that case. "Personal interest" includes a financial interest in the outcome, a close personal or business relation with the parties, or a predetermined opinion about the outcome. Having some opinions about the matter does not disqualify a member, but if those opinions rise to the level of a fixed opinion that is not susceptible to change ("My mind is made up, don't confuse me with the facts"), then the member should be disqualified.

The usual practice is for the member with a disqualifying conflict to state that he or she has a conflict and will not be participating. If there is a dispute over whether a conflict exists, the chair can make a ruling and the chair's ruling is subject to appeal to the full board (state law is not entirely clear on this point, so a clear procedure in the board's own rules of procedure is advisable). Whenever a member is disqualified, that member should not participate in the hearing in any way, neither asking questions, nor debating, nor voting on the case. It is a good practice, though not legally required, for a member with a conflict of interest to physically leave the room while that case is being handled by the board.

Record keeping. Complete records must be kept of the evidentiary hearings. Though not legally required to do so, many boards make audio tapes of the hearings in case a transcript is needed if the case is appealed to the courts. Detailed minutes must be kept noting the identity of witnesses and giving a complete summary of their testimony. Any exhibits presented should be retained by the board and become a part of the file on that case.

Open meetings. The state's open meetings law applies to boards making quasi-judicial decisions. This means that the regular meeting schedule must be filed with the city or county clerk, additional notice is required for special meetings, and all of the hearing and the board's deliberations must be conducted in open, public session. The board may not go into a closed session to discuss the case after receiving the evidence.

Findings. After taking evidence, the board must make written findings of fact. This is necessary to let the parties—and, if the matter is appealed, the courts—know what the board concluded about the facts of the case. Proposed findings can be drafted ahead of time and adopted at the meeting or findings can be composed at the conclusion of the hearing. The courts have ruled that there must be "substantial, competent, and material evidence" in the record to support each critical finding. This means key points need to be substantiated by the factual evidence in the hearing record; the findings cannot be based on conjecture or assumptions. For example, for the board to find that neighboring property values would be significantly reduced by a proposed project, there must be some testimony in the record to support that finding, such as testimony from a Realtor about the impacts of a similar project elsewhere in town.

Once a decision is made, a formal written copy must be mailed to the applicant and mailed to those present at the hearing who made a written request for a copy, and a formal copy must be filed with the city or county office specified in the ordinance.

Voting. State statutes impose a special voting requirement for most quasi-judicial decisions. A four-fifths vote rather than a simple majority is required in order for a zoning board of adjustment or planning board to grant a variance, issue a special-use permit, or overturn a zoning administrator's determination. If the city council or county board of commissioners is the decision-making body for special- or conditional-use permits, however, a simple majority vote suffices. A "four-fifths vote" means four-fifths of the entire board must vote in favor of the proposal, not just four-fifths of those present and voting. In the case of a ten-member board of adjustment with two members absent, a unanimous, eight-to-zero vote would be necessary. This is one reason most boards of adjustment have alternate members who can take an absent or disqualified member's place.

Rehearings. Once a final decision is reached on a quasi-judicial zoning decision, it is not proper to bring the same matter back to the board for a rehearing. Unless there is a different application or conditions have changed on the site or in the ordinance, a board does not have the legal authority to rehear such cases.

Appeals. Appeals of quasi-judicial decisions go directly to court. An applicant may not appeal a board of adjustment's decision to the governing board.

Suppose a town sets up its zoning ordinance so that the city council makes final decisions on special-use permits. Because these elected officials are the ones who adopted the ordinance and set the standards for special-use permits in the first place, surely they do not have to go through all of the formalities of putting folks under oath, taking evidence, and making written findings when they rule on permit applications, right? Wrong. As the town council in Chapel Hill found out, the courts require that whoever grants conditional-use or special-use permits must follow all of the rules for a fair evidentiary hearing.

In the fall of 1970, the Humble Oil Company obtained options on property at the far west end of Franklin Street in Chapel Hill, near the town's border with Carrboro. Part of the property was vacant, part had two small houses, and part was a used-car lot. The company proposed clearing the property and putting in an automobile service station. The

Figure 18. The car lot above was the site of the proposed gasoline station involved in the *Humble Oil* litigation. It remained a used-car lot for over twenty years after the landowners won their case.

town's appearance commission approved the project and the application for a special-use permit then went to a joint hearing by the town council and the planning board. Seven persons appeared and briefly spoke against the proposal, all in very general terms. The minister of a nearby church felt the gas station would be a traffic problem unless traffic lights were installed. Another speaker objected to removal of a tree. Several others expressed the opinion that there were already too many gas stations downtown. One speaker simply said she opposed the project. Hearing these concerns, the town council decided on the spot not to refer the case to the planning board for a recommendation, then unanimously voted to deny the permit on the basis of potential traffic problems. The company sued, contending its constitutional right to a fair hearing had been denied.

The North Carolina Supreme Court agreed with the applicant. The court held that whenever a special- or conditional-use permit decision is made, whoever makes that decision must abide by all of the rules for a fair hearing—sworn testimony, cross-examination, adequate evidence in the record to support the decision, and written findings of fact. Since the only information on traffic hazards in the record was the lay opinion of a minister, the court ruled the town council had not complied with the standards for a fair hearing. The court sent the case back to the town for a new hearing and decision.

So, did the Humble Oil Company then get to build its gas station? No. By the time the case was returned to the city in January 1974, a gasoline shortage had emerged. Existing stations were only able to open a few days a week, so the applicant did not pursue the matter. The lot (see Figure 18, page 53) remained a used-car lot for the next twenty years. However, in 1995, the town did issue a special-use permit for a quick-oil-change business on the site, thus an automobile service facility may finally come to this spot in Chapel Hill. This time the town's approval was conditioned on inclusion of some additional street-oriented retail use (such as a shop or a restaurant) in the project and a low brick wall to screen the parking. By the way, traffic lights at both corners were installed long before the second application came along. The same minister was still serving the nearby church, but neither he nor others raised objections this time around.

Special-Use Permits

Many zoning ordinances set up a category for uses that are not automatically permitted in a particular zoning district, but are permitted if certain specified conditions are met. A permit may be granted for such a use after an evidentiary hearing finds the specified conditions fulfilled. Such a permit may be called a *special-use permit*, a *conditional-use permit*, or a *special exception* (the terms are legally the same and are interchangeable). A special-use permit might, for example, provide that duplexes, normally not allowed in a single-family residential district, are permissible anywhere in that district but only upon a determination that (1) they are located on a lot that contains at least 20,000 square feet, (2) there is sufficient road frontage for two driveways at least 50 feet apart, and (3) the unit is designed to appear compatible with the surrounding houses.

The decisions on permit applications may be made by the planning board, the board of adjustment, or the governing board. Each local government specifies the decision-making body in its zoning ordinance. It is possible to assign some of these decisions to one board and some to a different board. Often, if a zoning ordinance splits the decisions on such permits between two boards, each board will use a different name for the permit it grants to reduce confusion. For example, the permits granted by the governing board may be called "special-use permits" and those granted by the planning board, "conditional-use permits."

The zoning ordinance itself must spell out requirements for granting such permits. The decision may not be left to the unfettered discretion of the board making the decision, even if it is the governing board. Likewise, extremely general requirements, such as that the project be in the public interest or that it be consistent with the purposes of the ordinance, are not adequate. Many ordinances use a combination of general and specific standards, though both are not legally required. Examples of general standards include requirements that the project not materially endanger public health and safety, that the project not substantially injure the value of adjoining property, that the project be in harmony with the surrounding area, and that the use be in conformance with the comprehensive plan. Specific standards may include minimum lot sizes, buffering or landscaping requirements, special setbacks, and the like.

The burden is on the applicant to present sufficient evidence to allow the board to make a finding that all of the required specific standards will be met. If insufficient evidence is presented, the permit must be denied. If uncontradicted evidence is presented that all of the standards will be met, the board must issue the permit. If there is conflicting evidence, the board decides what the facts are and either issues or denies the permit. The board can impose additional conditions on the permit if needed to bring the project into compliance with the standards in the ordinance. It can place an expiration date on a special-use permit as well, so that if a building permit for the project is not secured within a certain time, the permit expires. Once issued, the permit can be transferred by the applicant to another person, but not to another property. The permit applies to the property involved, not to the person receiving it. For this reason, some local governments require that special-use permits be recorded in the chain of title so that future purchasers of a property will be fully aware of any permit provisions.

Variances

One of the most powerful and difficult quasi-judicial zoning decisions is the *variance*. Since zoning ordinances were first drafted in the 1920s, the variance has been available as a safety valve for unusual, unanticipated situations. The underlying notion of the variance is that a governing board cannot possibly anticipate every circumstance that will arise in the implementation of zoning and that an administrative tool short of amending the ordinance is needed to deal with these peculiar situations. The variance is an important tool that allows the local government to avoid an unconstitutional taking of a person's property (see Chapter 9 for more on that topic) or an unintended inequity in the application of the ordinance. For example, a zoning board of adjustment might grant a variance to allow a house to be built ten feet from the side property line instead of the required twenty feet because steep slopes prevent building elsewhere on the lot. Variances are almost always handled by a board of adjustment, but as with other quasi-judicial decisions, each local government has the flexibility to assign these to other citizen boards.

The applicant for a variance comes to the city or county with a proposal along these lines: "My project is inconsistent with your zoning requirements. However, what I want to do is consistent with what you are trying to accomplish with the ordinance and would have been allowed had this been considered when the ordinance was adopted. Because of these peculiar circumstances, you are justified in allowing me some relief from the requirements of your zoning ordinance." Granting an individual an exemption from the legal requirements that apply to everyone else in the city or county goes contrary to the usual presumption that the law must apply to everyone equally. Thus the courts have imposed some fairly strict requirements on variances to make sure this tool is not abused.

The zoning statutes allow variance requests to be considered only when the board concludes that "practical difficulties or unnecessary hardships" would result from a strict application of the zoning requirements. If a person can comply with zoning requirements, the fact that they do not want to comply or that it is inconvenient or costly to comply is not a legitimate basis for a variance petition. The applicant must show some real difficulty and unnecessary hardship. Determining how large a hardship has to be before it becomes "unnecessary" is a case-by-case judgment—perhaps the single most difficult task for many boards handling variance requests. There is simply no hard and fast rule that can be laid down for making these decisions. However, courts around the country have provided a number of tests to be considered: no reasonable use can be made of the property without the variance; the hardship must result from the application of the terms of the ordinance itself; the hardship must be related to the physical property, not the condition of the applicant; the hardship must not be of the applicant's own making; and the hardship must be peculiar to the specific property involved.

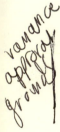

Further, the variance can be granted only if the spirit of the ordinance is observed, public safety and welfare are secured, and substantial justice is done. This limits the scope of legally permissible variances. It is not legal, for instance, to issue a variance to allow a land use that is clearly not allowed in a particular zoning district, such as a business use in an exclusively residential zoning district. Such an unpermitted use cannot be consistent with the spirit and intent of the ordinance. So if someone wants to undertake a use not allowed by the zoning ordinance, he or she must ask for an amendment to the ordinance rather than a variance. Similarly, variances cannot be issued to extend or expand *nonconformities*, those land uses in place before the adoption of a zoning requirement that do not comply with that requirement. They also may not be issued for projects that would create a nuisance.

As with special- or conditional-use permits, individual variances can be made subject to conditions. For example, the board may grant a variance to allow a parking area to be located closer than usual to the side property line, but may add a condition that a fence or vegetated buffer be provided to screen the site.

Appeals

Most zoning ordinances allow citizens to appeal administrative zoning decisions to a citizen board, typically the board of adjustment. This appeal system provides a quicker, more expert review than would be the case if persons had to go directly to the courts to challenge such a decision. Such appeals may contest zoning officer decisions about whether a particular use is allowed in a particular zoning district or a proposed sign complies with the restrictions in the ordinance.

The appeals system applies only to staff decisions or interpretations. A citizen whose proposal has been denied by one citizen board on a quasi-judicial matter under normal circumstances cannot appeal to a different citizen board. This kind of appeal must go to the courts. For example, if an affected party is dissatisfied with the decision of the planning board on a special-use permit, that party cannot appeal the decision to the board of adjustment or the city council. This kind of appeal must go to the courts.

Also, boards are not to issue advisory decisions on appeals. Only formal staff decisions or rulings may be appealed to the board. The state statutes do not specify how quickly an appeal must be filed with the board after the staff decision is made. If the local ordinance establishes a time limit, that period will be binding, but will start to run only after notice of the zoning officer's decision has been given to the applicant. If no set time is established, the appeal must be filed within a reasonable time.

Judicial Review

Once a final decision has been rendered on any of these quasi-judicial zoning decisions, a person who is directly affected by the decision can appeal that decision to superior court in the county where the decision was made. Such an appeal to the court must be filed within thirty days of the date notice of the final decision is mailed to the parties and officially filed with the city or county, whichever is later.

The superior court does not conduct a new hearing to determine the facts. Rather, it sits as an appeals court and bases its decision on the factual record established at the evidentiary hearing conducted by the local citizen board. This is one of the reasons it is important that adequate evidence be presented at the board hearing and that good records be kept of those proceedings. Probably the most frequent reason a citizen board's quasi-judicial zoning decision is overruled by the courts is that there was inadequate evidence in the record to support the board's findings of fact.

Other factors considered by the courts when they review these zoning decisions are whether proper procedures were followed in the decision-making process, whether there were errors made in interpreting the law, and whether the decision was "arbitrary and capricious." On this latter point, the court may not substitute its judgment for that of the citizen board; it does not second-guess a close call or consider whether the citizen board made the "right" decision. But if there is no rational basis for the decision, the court can overturn it.

7 Administrative Decisions and Zoning Enforcement

City and county staff play a vital role in the day-to-day administration of local zoning programs. The staff is generally responsible for processing routine permit applications, providing support to the various citizen boards involved, maintaining accurate records, and handling zoning enforcement. Much of this work is done by the zoning administrator and staff zoning inspectors (collectively called *zoning officers*). Planners, clerks, and other office personnel also play important roles, but the focus of this chapter is on the zoning officers who issue permits, make site inspections, and handle zoning enforcement actions. This chapter provides an overview of these responsibilities.

The Zoning Officers

Each zoning ordinance designates a city or county staff person as the *zoning administrator*. In most local governments in North Carolina, this responsibility is assigned to an inspections department, although it can be assigned to a planning department or some other department within the city or county government. Some smaller cities contract with another local government or even a private contractor to provide these administrative services. Or, a county and several cities may set up a joint inspections and enforcement department. Each local ordinance must specify who has responsibility for zoning administration, but the statutes allow substantial flexibility in just where that responsibility is housed.

The zoning administrator is a public officer of the local government and, as an "officer" instead of an "employee," has certain powers, duties, and protections. The administrator must take an oath of office, swearing or affirming to support the constitution and laws and to faithfully carry out his or her duties. Zoning officers working under the administrator also have decision-making authority, and must also take the oath of office. The oath of office is administered at the time the officer assumes his or her duties. It should not be confused with the oath to testify truthfully that is administered each time the officer presents testimony in a hearing.

Zoning officers have some immunity from suits related to carrying out their official duties. As a general rule, a zoning officer does not have personal financial liability for good-faith mistakes made in carrying out his or her duties. Liability for officers is limited to intentional wrongdoing (such as assaulting an applicant); corrupt and malicious acts (such as intentionally denying a permit solely because of a personal vendetta against the applicant); or negligence in carrying out routine, nondiscretionary acts (such as running through a stoplight and causing an accident while driving to a site to conduct an inspection or filing a plan).

The local government unit is also generally immune from liability. The government's immunity can be waived by the purchase of liability insurance, something many North Carolina cities and counties have done. The waiver is, however, limited to the amount of insurance coverage purchased by the local government.

Duties of the Zoning Officers

The zoning administrator and zoning staff persons have a number of important duties. They process all applications (see Figure 19). They make application forms available to the public, explain the ordinance requirements to the public, and review applications to verify the information they contain and assess the application's compliance with the terms of the zoning ordinance. Zoning officers issue all routine permits. If an application involves both fact-finding and the application of discretionary standards, such as with a conditional-use permit or a special-use permit, the decision must be made by a citizen board rather than a zoning officer.

The zoning officers are responsible for making inspections during and at the conclusion of the permitted work to assure that the zoning requirements have been met. Zoning officers also perform routine tasks for the citizen boards, including preparing reports, assuring proper notice of meetings, and filing the decisions made. The city or county clerk and the planning staff often share responsibility for these administrative duties. Zoning officers investigate complaints and initiate all enforcement actions when violations are discovered.

The zoning administrator is also responsible for maintaining all appropriate zoning records. Files must be maintained on all applications and permit decisions. Records of enforcement actions and decisions by citizens boards on permits, appeals, variances, and ordinance changes must be maintained. These materials are public records and must be made available for public inspection during normal business hours.

Zoning Enforcement

The first step in zoning enforcement is inspection of potential violations. Inspections are usually triggered by citizen complaints, but the staff may also conduct routine inspections. A zoning officer must have the

ZONING CLEARANCE FOR BUILDING PERMIT APPLICATION

GENERAL INFORMATION

Job Address _____ Tax Map No. _____

Owner _____ Zoning _____

Flood Plain _____

Contractor _____ Contact Person _____

Address _____ Phone Number _____

Lincense No. _____ Priv. License _____ Sq. Ft. _____

Type of Application: ____addition ____new construction ____other _____

Estimated Cost _____

SPECIFIC ZONING REQUIREMENTS

	MIN	ACTUAL		MIN	ACTUAL
Lot Size	____ ____	Parking Spaces		
Lot Width	____ ____	# Spaces	____ ____
Setbacks:		Handicapped	____ ____
Front Yard	____ ____		
Rear Yard	____ ____		
Right Yard	____ ____	Signs	
Left Yard	____ ____	Ground	____ ____
		Flush Mounted	____ ____
Minimum Combined Side Yard	____ ____		
% of Lot Coverage	____ ____		

REQUIRED INFORMATION (must be submitted to the Inspections Department when making application for a building permit along with 3 sets of complete building plans) and an approved erosion control plan, if greater than one (1) acre.

____ Site Plan Showing:

____ Lot Dimensions   ____ Easements

____ Structure Size & Location   ____ Parking Layout

____ Set Backs   ____ Flood Elevation Certification

____ Front Yard   ____ Number of Employees

____ Rear Yard   ____ Other (specify)

____ Left Yard   ____ Erosion Control Plan

____ Right Yard   (approved by North Carolina NRCD)

_____   _____

Signature of Applicant   Zoning Officer

pg 26

THIS FORM AND ABOVE REQUIRED INFORMATION MUST BE PRESENTED TO THE INSPECTION DEPARTMENT

Figure 19. The zoning officer processes a number of applications. These include verification that the zoning ordinance has been complied with (sample application form above is from the City of Statesville, North Carolina), sign permits, special- and conditional-use permits, variances, rezoning requests, and many others.

permission of the landowner to go onto private property to inspect areas that cannot be viewed from off the premises. If there are reasonable grounds to believe there may be a violation and permission is not granted, a zoning officer can obtain an administrative search warrant from a magistrate or judge that will authorize a reasonable inspection (see Figure 20, page 62).

STATE OF NORTH CAROLINA
In the General Court of Justice

_____ County

ADMINISTRATIVE INSPECTION WARRANT FOP PARTICULAR CONDITION OR ACTIVITY

G.S. 1   .2

TO ANY LAWFUL OFFICIAL EMPOWERED TO CONDUCT THE INSPECTION AUTHORIZED BY THIS WARRANT:

The applicant named on the accompanying affidavit, being duly sworn, has stated to me that there is a condition, object, activity, or circumstance legally justifying an inspection of the property described in that affidavit. I have examined this applicant under oath or affirmation and have verified the accuracy of the matters in the affidavit establishing the legal grounds for this warrant. YOU ARE HEREBY COMMANDED TO INSPECT THE PROPERTY DESCRIBED IN THE ACCOMPANYING AFFIDAVIT.

This inspection is authorized to check or reveal the conditions, objects, activities, or circumstances indicated in the accompanying affidavit.

This warrant must be served upon the owner or possessor of the property described in the accompanying affidavit. If the owner or possessor is not present on the property at the time of inspection and you have made reasonable but unsuccessful efforts to locate the owner or possessor, you may instead serve it by affixing this warrant or a copy to the property.

THIS WARRANT MAY BE EXECUTED ONLY BETWEEN THE HOURS OF 8:00 A.M. AND 8:00 P.M. AND ONLY WITHIN 24 HOURS AFTER IT WAS ISSUED. IT MUST BE RETURNED WITHIN 48 HOURS AFTER IT WAS ISSUED. HOWEVER, IF THIS WARRANT IS ISSUED PURSUANT TO A FIRE INVESTIGATION AUTHORIZED BY G.S. 69-1, IT MAY BE EXECUTED AT ANY TIME WITHIN 48 HOURS AFTER IT IS ISSUED. IT MUST RETURNED WITHOUT UNNECESSARY DELAY AFTER ITS EXECUTION OR AFTER 48 HOURS FROM THE TI IT WAS ISSUED IF IT WAS NOT EXECUTED.

Date	Time	□ A.M. □ P.M.
Signature		

□ Assistant CSC   □ Deputy CSC   □ Clerk of Superior Court
□ Magistrate   □ Superior Court Judge   □ District Court Judge

OFFICER'S RETURN

I certify that this WARRANT was executed on the date and time shown below.

Date of Execution	Signature of Inspecting Official
Time of Execution □ A.M. □ P.M.	

CLERK'S ACCEPTANCE

This WARRANT has been returned to this office on the date and time shown below.

Date of return	Signature
Time of return □ A.M. □ P.M.	□ Assistant CSC □ Deputy CSC □ Clerk of Superior Court

AOC-CR-913M, Side Two
Rev. 7-85

IMPORTANT: Attach Affidavit to Warrant if not on reverse side.

Figure 20. After presenting an affidavit to a judge or magistrate setting forth the reasons to believe a zoning violation exists, a zoning officer can be issued an administrative search warrant, such as the one pictured above. It authorizes a reasonable inspection during regular business hours. The inspection must be made within forty-eight hours of the issuance of the warrant. Other warrants are available for periodic inspections such as those done over the continuing course of construction.

If the zoning officer determines that there has been a violation of the zoning ordinance, he or she sends a written notice to the owner of the property. Notice may also be sent to the occupant if that is a different person. Such notice generally identifies the nature of the violation and directs the owner to bring the site into compliance within a set time. If the zoning officer determines that there is work under way that is in substantial violation of the zoning ordinance or that is dangerous, the zoning officer can issue a formal *stop work order* (see Figure 21, page 64). A stop work order must be in writing; it must specify the violation found; and it must tell the person what he or she must do to be able to resume work. Stop work orders can be appealed to the board of adjustment.

The zoning officer also has the option of revoking any permits that are being violated, whether or not a stop work order has been issued. A permit revocation must be in writing and it can be appealed to the board of adjustment. The statutes provide that a building permit *must* be revoked in three instances: (1) when there is a substantial departure from approved plans; (2) when there is a failure to comply with the zoning ordinance; and, (3) when there are false statements on the application. A permit *may* be revoked if it was mistakenly issued.

Following the notice of violation, and issuance of a stop work order or revocation of a building permit, local governments have three additional legal tools for zoning enforcement.

1. Civil penalties. If the local zoning ordinance specifically authorizes civil penalties for violations, the local zoning administrator may assess such a penalty. The amount of the civil penalty must be reasonably related to the amount of harm caused by the violation and the cost to the local government of securing compliance. The ordinance can provide that each day of continuing violation after notice of violation is a separate offense. The assessment of a civil penalty can generally be appealed to the board of adjustment.

2. Criminal prosecution. Violation of a zoning ordinance is a misdemeanor and can be prosecuted as a criminal offense. Current state law makes violation of a local zoning ordinance a misdemeanor, punishable by a fine of up to $200 as specified in the ordinance. (The maximum fine is $50 if the ordinance does not specify a higher amount.) If the person has five or more prior convictions, the sentence may include a jail term of up to twenty days.

3. Injunctions or court orders. The local government can get an injunction or court order to compel compliance. To secure an injunction, the city or county must first file a lawsuit to ask a judge to take this action. This kind of action is used only in extreme cases, such as where the violation presents a threat to public health or safety or the other enforcement tools have been tried and have failed to secure compliance. Violation of a court order to comply subjects the violator to contempt of court

**DURHAM CITY-COUNTY
INSPECTIONS DEPARTMENT**
101 CITY HALL PLAZA
DURHAM, N.C. 27701
(919) 560-4144
FAX 560-4484

STOP WORK ORDER

To:

Re:

In accordance with the authority contained in the North Carolina State Building Code (Section 2.3 of Volume I-A and Section R-107.3 of Volume VII), as well as G.S. 153A-361 and G.S. 160A-421 of the North Carolina General Statutes, you are hereby ordered to stop all _____ work immediately on the structure at the above referenced address.

This order is being issued because _____
_____. Work may not proceed until
_____.

Sincerely,

Code Enforcement Official

Received By: _____

Witnessed By: _____

Date: _____

AN EQUAL OPPORTUNITY/AFFIRMATIVE ACTION EMPLOYER

Figure 21. A zoning official can issue a stop work order to halt construction on a project that is in violation of a zoning ordinance.

sanctions, which can be severe—a violator may be held in jail until compliance is secured.

As a general rule, the decision on whether to initiate an enforcement action is left to the discretion and judgment of the zoning administrator. Zoning officers do have a duty to make a reasonable investigation of credible complaints, but there is no mandate that any particular enforcement action must result from an investigation. The fact that a similar prior violation by someone else has not been prosecuted is not a valid defense on the part of a person charged with a zoning violation. Only in extreme instances would selective enforcement be a valid defense to an alleged zoning violation.

If zoning officers do investigate and discover a violation but then there is a considerable delay before any enforcement action is taken, the courts have the option of refusing to allow enforcement. If the length of the delay is unreasonable and the delayed enforcement would put the violator at an unreasonable disadvantage, a court can find the delayed enforcement unfair and thus invalid.

8 Special Consideration for Existing Development

Once a zoning ordinance or amendment is adopted, the expectation is that it will apply equally to everyone. This notion of equal treatment of all persons is an important part of our legal system. Zoning ordinances are not, however, applied to a blank slate. In a real community, there are developments already in place that are inconsistent with the zoning adopted for future development, such as a preexisting store located in an area zoned for residential uses. Other developments may have been approved under an old zoning ordinance but be only partially completed when new requirements become effective.

Both the courts and most zoning ordinances make special provisions for existing and partially completed developments. The courts do this through the *vested rights* concept, a doctrine that provides that once a person has established a legal right to carry out a project, it can be done under the rules that were in effect when the project was approved. Zoning ordinances also usually include provisions to handle *nonconformities*, preexisting developments that do not match current zoning. Such provisions allow nonconformities to remain in place with limits as to future expansion. This chapter addresses these concepts.

Vested Rights

The process of moving from an idea to develop property to the point where the development is actually finished and in use takes time. At some point in this process, the owner obtains a legal right to continue to develop even if the rules regarding the development change. When this right is obtained, the owner is said to have a "vested right," the legal right to complete the development under the terms of the original approval.

In North Carolina land-use law, there are three kinds of vested rights. The first has been established by the courts: the *common-law vested right*. The second was established by the legislature in 1985: the *building permit vested right*. The third was established by the legislature in 1990: the *site-specific development plan vested right*. The means to obtain these rights are summarized in Figure 22 (page 68). These three means of securing vested rights are not mutually exclusive. A person can have a building permit vested right that later becomes a common-law vested right once substantial work is started on the project.

Type of Vested Right	Requirements	Duration
Common-law vested right	Substantial expenditure of time, effort, or money in good-faith reliance on valid governmental approval.	Indefinite.
Building permit vested right	A valid, current building permit for the project.	Generally lasts only six months unless work actually starts.
Site-specific development plan vested right	A public hearing on the project, followed by local government approval of a "site-specific development plan" as defined in the zoning ordinance.	Lasts at least two years; local ordinance may extend to up to five years.

Figure 22. Requirements to obtain vested rights.

Common-Law Vested Right

The common-law vested right is based on the simple principle of fairness. If a person comes to the government and gets approval to develop a project and then, in reliance on that approval, takes substantial steps to carry out the project, it would be unfair to make the person comply with newly adopted standards if doing so would cause some significant hardship to that person. In a long series of cases the courts have developed rules for determining if and when a common-law vested right has been established. The rule is that the owner must have made substantial expenditures in good faith reliance on a valid governmental approval in order to have a common-law vested right. Each of the following individual requirements must be met.

1. Obtain valid governmental approval. The first step in securing a common-law vested right is obtaining a valid governmental approval of a specific project. An owner cannot obtain a vested right from the ordinance itself, only the specific governmental approval of an individual project triggers this legal right. For example, an investor may carefully review the zoning ordinance to identify land zoned for commercial uses and then, relying on the ordinance, buy commercially zoned land, paying a substantial price for that land. But if the investor takes no action to get specific governmental approval to actually develop the site for a commercial use, and the local government subsequently rezones the land to residential use, the investor has no vested rights to commercial use of the property. "Specific governmental approval" can consist of a certificate of zoning compliance for a permitted use, a special- or conditional-use permit, a subdivision plat approval, a building permit, or some other required approval. The approval that is received must be valid at the time received—vested rights cannot be based on a mistakenly or illegally granted permit. The requirement of specific governmental approval is waived only if no permit was required for the proposed development and the owner was proceeding in an entirely lawful manner. In such a case, a common-law vested right can be established if the other parts of the rule are met.

2. Make a substantial expenditure. The second step in securing a common-law vested right is to make some substantial expenditure based on specific governmental approval. The expenditure can be of time, effort, or money. Actual construction is not necessary. The expenditure must be "substantial" in relation to the overall expenditure required to carry out the project. For example, simply going to the site and making some modest site clearing or construction may not be "substantial" expenditure for a large commercial project, but a few hours' work toward installing a billboard may be sufficient if that brings the job close to completion. If the project is being carried out in several phases, the vested right will apply only to those phases for which the expenditures have actually been made.

3. Act in good faith. Equity and fairness must be considered: the owner must have been acting in good faith. If it is apparent that the owner was deceiving or misleading the government or neighbors, or the owner was acting outside of normal business practices, such as moving with undue haste in order to beat a rule change, a vested right is not established.

4. Suffer harm. The owner must show that he or she would be harmed if required to comply with the new rules. If all of the expenditures made under the original approval can be applied just as well to a project that complies with the new rules, there is no vested right to develop under the old rules.

The two remaining vested rights were created by the legislature in an attempt to bring greater certainty and simplicity to this question.

Building Permit Vested Right

The building permit vested right became a provision of the zoning enabling statutes in 1985 in G.S. 153A-344(b) and G.S. 160A-385(b). It provides that as long as a valid building permit is outstanding, the owner has a vested right to complete the development authorized by that permit. There is no requirement that any expenditures be made in reliance on the building permit. The permit involved here is not just any permit; it must be the building permit required under the state building code. These building permits expire six months after issuance if work has not commenced. They also expire after work commences if there is a twelve-month period of no work. Building permits may also be revoked for any substantial departure from the approved plans, failure to comply with any applicable state or local law (not just the building code and zoning ordinance), and any misrepresentations made in securing the permit. Building permits mistakenly issued may also be revoked. If the building permit expires or is revoked, the vested right based on it is also lost.

Site-Specific Development Plan Vested Right

The second statutory vested right is related to the *site-specific development plan* and was added to the statutes in 1990 to deal with more complex development projects (G.S. 153A-344.1 and G.S. 160A-385.1). Each local government is allowed to establish in its zoning ordinance its own definition of what constitutes a site-specific development plan. For the purposes of securing a vested right, a "site plan" is not the same thing as a "site-specific development plan." Site-specific development plans may include preliminary plats under subdivision ordinances as well as conditional- and special-use permits. If the local zoning ordinance itself does not define site-specific development plans, an owner can use a zoning permit to qualify. The local government conducts a hearing before approving the plan. This should probably be an evidentiary hearing, but the statutes are unclear on this point. Once the plan is approved, the owner's vested right is established; the owner is exempt from any future zoning changes that affect the type or intensity of development that has already been approved. In a variation on this process, owners can submit and local governments can approve a more general *phased development plan* that gives this same type of vested right for up to five years. A phased development plan is a more general depiction of proposed development over a longer time period.

Local governments can also allow completion of ongoing projects when amending their ordinances by postponing the effective date of the amendment or by providing that it applies only to applications received after a certain date. Whether or not to do this is a policy choice for the governing board.

Nonconformities

When zoning ordinances are adopted, they usually contain provisions that allow continuation of existing development that is inconsistent with the terms of the new ordinance. Such developments are called *nonconformities*. Protections may extend to several types of nonconformities:

a nonconforming use, such as a business in a residential district; a nonconforming lot, such as one that is smaller than the minimum allowed in a particular district; or a nonconforming structure, such as one that is too close to the rear property line. A nonconformity must have been legal when it was initiated to receive protection. A use that was a zoning violation when it started does not ripen into a legitimate nonconformity no matter how long it has been there. If there is a dispute as to when the nonconformity was established or what its scope is, the zoning administrator makes a ruling on the question. Appeals of that ruling can be taken to the board of adjustment.

The usual practice is to allow nonconformities to continue but to place limitations on them. The scope of these limitations varies with each ordinance. Most zoning ordinances limit nonconformities with the intent of eventually phasing them out or at least keeping them from getting any worse. A typical restriction is that a nonconforming building cannot be enlarged, expanded, or extended. Another is that a nonconforming use cannot be resumed if it has been abandoned or discontinued for a specified period (typically six or twelve months). There are often restrictions on repairs of nonconforming structures. Routine maintenance and minor repairs are usually allowed, but substantial repairs or replacement are not. The ordinance also often prohibits the owner from changing one nonconforming use to a different nonconforming use.

These restrictions on nonconformities are legal and enforceable. However, if there is any doubt as to whether a restriction applies, the courts will resolve that doubt in favor of allowing the person to make use of the property as proposed. Therefore local governments should carefully consider just how restrictive they want the nonconforming limitations to be and define those limitations clearly in the ordinance.

In some limited circumstances, a local government can require a nonconformity to be terminated (removed), or force the owner to bring the use into compliance with the ordinance. If the nonconformity poses a threat to public health and safety, immediate termination is warranted. Otherwise, the owner must be given a reasonable time period to recoup his or her investment and make alternate plans before having to come into compliance. The practice of requiring inconsistent uses to be phased out or brought into compliance after a defined grace period is called *amortization*. For example, a billboard owner may be given five years to use a nonconforming billboard but at the end of the amortization period it must be brought into compliance (such as replacing it with a smaller sign if that is allowed or removing it altogether). The amortization period allowed must be reasonable in light of the owner's investment in the nonconformity, the income it generates, its salvage value, and the like. The amortization tool has been applied most often in North Carolina to signs, junkyards, and adult entertainment uses.

Jurisdictions can phase out nonconformities through amortization, but sometimes these uses turn out to be quite persistent. The North Carolina court case that established the law on amortization is a good example.

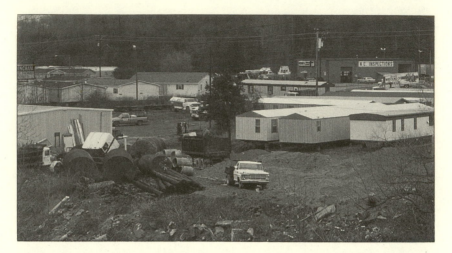

Figure 23. Joyner's salvage yard in 1993. Twenty-five years after the courts upheld the legality of Winston-Salem's ordinance requiring removal of Joyner's junkyard, it was still in operation. The city rezoned the site after the court case was concluded.

In 1966 Roy Joyner started a building salvage yard on property he leased in north Winston-Salem. A city zoning provision adopted in 1968 required this salvage yard to be removed within three years. Joyner contended it would cost him $25,000 to relocate and refused to comply. In 1973 the city cited him for a criminal violation of the zoning ordinance. At trial, the jury found him guilty, and this verdict was upheld by both the North Carolina and United States supreme courts. The state supreme court decision, written by Justice Dan Moore, concluded that amortization is legal so long as the time period allowed to come into compliance is reasonable.

So, after all of this lengthy legal wrangling and a trip to the highest courts, what happened to Joyner's salvage yard? It is still in business on the same site (see Figure 23). After the city won in court, it agreed to rezone the property to a district that would allow continuation of the salvage yard.

9 Constitutional Limits on Zoning

The power of local governments to regulate land use and development through zoning is subject to the limits imposed by the state and federal constitutions. Any zoning action that is inconsistent with these limits can be declared unconstitutional by the courts and invalidated. A local government undertaking an unconstitutional action may also be subject to financial liability. Most people do not think of zoning regulations in the same breath as constitutional protections, but there are constitutional limits on zoning and it is important to understand them. As one U.S. Supreme Court justice remarked in reviewing the constitutionality of a land-use regulation, "After all, if a policeman must know the Constitution, then why not a planner?"

There are four major limits on the zoning power imposed by the United States Constitution. These are: (1) the restrictions imposed by the *Due Process Clause* that governmental actions be fundamentally fair; (2) the requirement of the *Equal Protection Clause* that persons in similar situations be treated alike by the law; (3) the protections provided by the First Amendment to *freedom of speech and religion*; (4) the limitation of the *taking clause of the Fifth Amendment* that private property not be taken for public use without compensation. This chapter will address each of these limitations.

Due Process

The Fifth and Fourteenth amendments to the United States Constitution provide that no person shall be deprived of life, liberty, or property without due process of law. A similar provision is in the North Carolina constitution. The courts have interpreted this requirement to impose two important limitations on zoning. First, zoning hearings and the decision-making process must be carried out fairly. Second, the substance of zoning actions must be reasonable.

The first requirement of procedural fairness is relatively straightforward. Its most important application in zoning is to the requirement that all hearings on quasi-judicial zoning matters—variances, special- and conditional-use permits, and appeals of zoning administrator determinations—be conducted in a fair and impartial manner. Since these quasi-judicial zoning decisions involve the determination of individual legal rights in a particular case, these proceedings must be conducted somewhat similarly to a court proceeding. While some informality is allowed, due process requires that all of the fundamental rights to a fair hearing be observed. This means that the applicant and other affected persons appearing at the hearing must be given an opportunity to present witnesses and documents. All parties have the right to inspect all the evidence being considered by the decision maker. They have the right to cross-examine witnesses at the hearings and to have the witnesses testify under oath. They have the right to have the decision made solely on the basis of evidence presented at the hearing. This means that board members may not discuss the matter with persons outside of the hearing. Parties have a right to written findings of fact if there are disputed facts in the case. They also have the right to an impartial decision maker. This means a board member with a financial interest in the outcome of the decision may not participate in making rezonings and other legislative zoning decisions. With quasi-judicial zoning decisions, board members may not participate in a matter involving someone with whom they have a close family or business relation, nor may they participate if they have a bias (defined as fixed opinion that is not susceptible to change upon hearing the facts at the hearing). These limits on board members are discussed in more detail in Chapter 6.

The other aspect of due process—that zoning be reasonable—is a bit more complicated. The courts have ruled that this requirement has two components. First, zoning must be based on *legitimate governmental objectives*. Second, there must be a *reasonable relationship* between the specific zoning restriction and these legitimate objectives.

1. Legitimate governmental objectives. In determining whether zoning is based on legitimate objectives, it is important that a city or county have completed solid technical studies and plans that can serve as the foundation for zoning decisions. These studies and plans should address the area's natural features, population changes, existing development, public service needs, and the like. Examples of legitimate objectives for zoning include protecting public health and safety; assuring adequate public utilities (including transportation, water, sewer, parks, and schools); protecting natural resources and open spaces, protecting community aesthetics and historic values, and conserving and protecting property values. The courts have ruled that zoning cannot be used to promote residential racial segregation, to control the ownership (as opposed to the use) of property, to enforce private restrictive covenants on property use or otherwise protect private rather than public interests.

2. Reasonable relation. There must also be a reasonable relation between the legitimate goals of zoning listed above and the zoning ordinance. In other words, each zoning restriction must be designed to achieve a legitimate objective. For example, if a city uses zoning to prohibit a drive-through window in a fast food restaurant because of traffic problems, but allows banks and other businesses in the same zoning district to have drive-through windows, the court may well conclude there is no reasonable relation between the end (preventing traffic problems) and the means chosen (limiting drive-through windows for some but not all businesses).

Due process also dictates that an ordinance restriction not be so vague that a person would not know what it does and does not require. If the standard required in a zoning ordinance is too general or imprecise, a court may invalidate it. For example, a requirement that signs not be "unattractive" or that a business not be "too noisy" would be too vague to pass constitutional muster.

Equal Protection

The Equal Protection Clause of the Fourteenth Amendment of the United States Constitution says that local governments cannot deny any person the equal protection of the law. This notion of the law applying evenhandedly is central to our legal system. Yet zoning ordinances clearly treat persons differently. What is permitted in one zoning district is prohibited in another district. A person who has already established a business in an area later zoned for residential use is allowed to stay, but someone else may be forbidden to open a new, similar business next door.

The Equal Protection Clause does not require everyone to be treated exactly the same by zoning. What it does require is that persons *in the same situation* be treated the same. So the key question becomes, When are people similarly situated? The courts allow there to be different development standards in different zoning districts because there has been a conclusion by the city council that different situations exist in different parts of the city. For example, one part of the city may be well suited for residential development so it is acceptable to zone it for residential use and impose standards suitable for a residential area that are different from the standards appropriate for an industrial area. Similarly, the person who had a development legally in place before zoning was adopted is in a different situation from the person wanting to develop after the ordinance is in place. Or, a church may be exempted from the off-street parking requirements that apply to a business because the church usually has a large parking demand only at times outside of normal business hours. In each of these instances of different treatment, the key is that there be a real and meaningful difference between the parties being treated differently.

A special cautionary note must be applied here. If a case-specific zoning restriction affects an owner's fundamental constitutionally protected right, such as the right of free speech, and that person takes the government to court to challenge the restrictions, the government must convince the court that there is a compelling reason for the special restriction, something that is almost impossible to do in a zoning context. For example, the Supreme Court said a city cannot prohibit news racks that sell sexually oriented papers while allowing similar news racks selling regular newspapers. The same exacting limitation applies to restrictions based on a constitutionally suspect classification, such as different treatment based on race, religion, or national origin. For example, a zoning restriction that limited occupancy in a particular residential district to a particular race would be invalid.

First Amendment

As noted above, the courts are very suspicious of zoning restrictions that limit First Amendment rights—freedom of religion, of speech, and of the press; the right to assemble peaceably; and the right to petition the government.

A free speech issue arises when local governments use zoning to regulate the adult entertainment business. For example, a county may attempt to ban "adult" bookstores but allow other bookstores, a distinction clearly based on the content of the books. The courts have ruled that special restrictions may be applied to businesses such as adult bookstores, topless bars, massage parlors, and the like. Importantly, special restrictions on such adult businesses are allowed only if the predominant purpose of the regulation is to address the secondary impacts of the activity rather than the activity itself. The local government may not simply conclude that the adult business is morally offensive and should be banned; it must base a zoning restriction on consideration of such factors as will promote the general welfare—protecting other retail trade, maintaining property values, protecting neighborhoods, preventing the spread of disease, preventing prostitution and other crime, preventing litter, and so on. The staff work supporting the zoning restriction needs to show how these considerations would be advanced by the proposal. A number of zoning restrictions on adult businesses have been upheld by the courts. For example, zoning ordinances can require that no more than one adult business or activity be located in a single building, that adult businesses be confined to certain zoning districts, that they be located a minimum distance from each other, or that they be located a minimum distance from other "sensitive uses," such as schools, churches, and residences. However, a complete zoning ban of lawful adult businesses is not allowed (because obscenity is a criminal offense addressed by laws other than zoning). After all of the restrictions on the location of adult businesses are considered, there must be a reasonable range of alternative sites left within the jurisdiction for their location. While the city does not have to act as a real estate agent to find a readily available alternative site, the city does need to conduct a study to assure that there are some sites realistically available for adult businesses before it adopts a particularly restrictive siting requirement for them.

The free speech issue also sometimes arises with sign regulations. The courts have traditionally allowed more substantial restrictions on "commercial speech," such as advertisements and signs, than on political or other speech. Ordinances can ban misleading or inaccurate advertisements. Other restrictions can be imposed that directly advance a substantial government interest (such as promoting traffic safety or preserving community aesthetic values). Such restrictions may be no more extensive than necessary to serve that interest. Under these standards, reasonable restrictions on commercial signs are clearly acceptable. Common regulations include limits on size, minimum separation between signs, prohibition of off-premise advertising, prohibition of billboards in certain zoning districts, and prohibition of all signs within a public right-of-way. However, particular care is needed when regulating noncommercial speech. The United States Supreme Court ruled, for example, that a city cannot completely prohibit political expressions on small signs placed in the window of a person's home. This is an evolving area of the law with a good deal of uncertainty as to just where the bounds of permissible regulation are. For that reason, sign regulations in some zoning ordinances completely exempt noncommercial speech.

The First Amendment also provides that government may not make a law prohibiting the free exercise of religion, and a federal statute extends this constitutional protection. As with limitations on free speech, a regulation based solely on religious grounds must be supported by a compelling governmental interest—something that would be almost impossible to establish in a zoning context. A zoning ordinance that prohibited a mosque but allowed a church in a particular zoning district would be invalid. This constitutional and statutory protection for free expression of religion is not an exemption from zoning for all aspects of religious land uses, however. The courts have held that legitimate regulations applying to other uses may be equally applied to religious uses. For example, requirements that a church provide space for off-street parking, that it secure a special-use permit for a homeless shelter or soup kitchen operated on church property, or that it limit sound from church bells or services to certain levels can be applied so long as they are also applied to all other uses as well.

Taking

The Fifth Amendment dictates that when private property is taken for public use, the owner must be fairly paid for the property. This was a simple proposition as long as it was applied to those instances where the government actually took title to or possession of private property, such as taking a person's land to build a road, a school, or a military base. Usually the only question in those instances was how much the land was worth and what would be just compensation.

The legal situation as it relates to zoning got considerably more complicated when the United States Supreme Court ruled in 1922 that a regulation that restricts property use could be so onerous that it has the same practical effect as a seizure of property. Thus, an individual property owner could not be singled out to bear a burden that should be borne by the public as a whole. Moving beyond this general concept to its application has proved difficult. This notion that an overly restrictive regulation can be a *taking* of property has become one of the most hotly contested and legally confusing areas of land-use law.

With more than a dozen United States Supreme Court decisions on this topic in the past twenty years, a few rules have emerged. First, a zoning restriction that requires a physical invasion of a person's property is automatically a taking. For example, zoning requirements that the public be allowed to use a private boat basin and that apartment building owners be required to allow cable TV wiring on their roof have both been held to be takings. Second, a regulation that renders a property *completely* worthless is a taking. Note that a severe reduction in value, such as might occur when a property is rezoned from a valuable commercial use to a less valuable residential use, is not itself a taking. For there to be an automatic taking, the regulation must remove all practical use of the property so that it has no reasonable value left.

If a case does not fit into one of these two rather narrow categories, the courts conduct an individual review of the case to determine if a regulation has gone too far and is thus unconstitutional. An important factor in these reviews is the economic impact on the person affected, with particular emphasis on the impact on "distinct investment backed expectations" (the courts have not yet clarified what this means). The character of the governmental action is also an important factor. A land-use restriction enacted to protect public health and safety is far less likely to be a taking than one adopted for improper purposes, such as to reduce the value of the property as a prelude to public purchase.

It is extremely unusual for the courts to hold that a zoning restriction is a taking. Most local governments reach the political limits of what they deem to be fair and reasonable well before they get close to the constitutional limits of the taking clause. But the uncertainty of the law in this area has provoked a great deal of controversy, debate, and litigation. There are also proposals in a number of states, North Carolina included, to adopt legislation that requires analysis of the taking issue prior to enactment of land-use regulations or that requires compensation for reductions in property values even if the regulation is not so onerous as to be an unconstitutional taking.

When a city rezones property to a more valuable use but later rezones it back to its original classification, can the property owner sue the city and recover compensation for change in property value?

This was the question presented by a recent Durham case. The dispute involved a 2.6-acre parcel near an interstate highway interchange. In 1947 the site was originally zoned for residential use. The immediately surrounding area was all single-family development, with the exception of a single abandoned gas station. There was commercial development across the interstate (see Figure 24, below). In 1979 Vernon Finch and some partners obtained an option to purchase the property and convinced the city council to rezone this property and the adjacent abandoned gas station from residential to commercial so they could build a 100-unit motel. After the property was rezoned to commercial use, the real estate market was a bit slow, so Finch took no immediate action to build. However, by late 1984 he had an agreement with Red Roof Inn to put a motel on the site. At that time he began the process of getting city approval.

In early 1985, as a first step to getting their building plans approved, the owners requested that the city close a street on the rear of the property. The neighbors learned of this and were very concerned about a motel being built in their neighborhood. In March 1985 several immediate neighbors and the neighborhood association asked the city to rezone the property back to its original, pre-1979, single-family residential use. In April the city's planning and zoning board held a public hearing on the request and recommended returning the zoning on the property to that of a residential district. In late April, before the city council considered

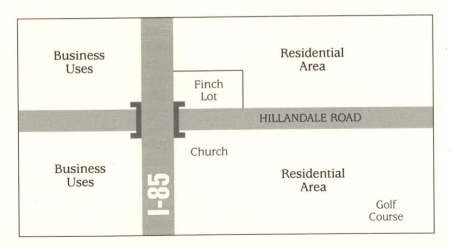

Figure 24. The site at issue in the *Finch* case.

Figure 25. This motel was originally proposed for the *Finch* site. It was eventually built a mile east of the site, on the other side of the interstate highway.

the matter, Finch had to decide whether to exercise the option to purchase the site. He decided to proceed and purchased the property for the agreed price of $165,000. In May the city council accepted the planning board recommendation and rezoned the property back to residential use. In June Finch entered into an agreement to sell the land to Red Roof Inn for $500,000, with the sale contingent on the property being zoned to allow a motel on the site. In November Mr. Finch sued the city.

While everyone agreed at the trial that the ordinance had considerably reduced the market value of the property, there was considerable dispute about the exact impact. The owners' experts contended the land was worth only $20,000 to $25,000 if zoned for residential use, figures considerably below the half-million dollars the owner could get if the property was zoned commercial. The city conceded the value was reduced, but contended the land with current zoning was worth at least $150,000. The jury ruled there was a taking but no damages. However, the trial judge then ruled that the city was liable for $151,000 in damages plus more than $61,000 for the owner's legal fees. When the case got to the North Carolina Supreme Court, the court overturned this judgment and held that even though there had been a very substantial reduction in value, this was *not* a taking of the owner's property because some practical use of the property with reasonable value was remaining.

After this case was decided, events continued to unfold. The entire site remained vacant for some years, while the proposed Red Roof Inn (see Figure 25) was built a half-mile away at the next interchange, which was zoned as a commercial area. In 1993, after several additional abortive attempts to secure more intensive zoning, the owner of the part of the site where the gas station used to be requested rezoning to a low-intensity office district and submitted a site plan for an office with detailed conditions regarding a landscaped buffer, parking, and street access. This project had the support of the neighborhood association. The city approved the rezoning and the real estate office (see Figure 26) was built on the site, a use certainly more compatible with the surrounding residential neighborhood than a large motel would have been. This type of practical compromise is not uncommon in zoning disputes. The portion of the site actually involved in the *Finch* litigation remains vacant.

Figure 26. This real estate office was eventually built on the property involved in the *Finch* case.

Two other areas of taking law warrant mention. The first is *amortization*, the practice of requiring nonconforming uses to be phased out or brought into compliance within a specified period. The courts in North Carolina have ruled that this is not a taking as long as a reasonable time period is allowed before requiring compliance. The length of the period should be based on the amount of the owner's investment in the use, the time it takes to recoup that investment, and the time needed to make alternative plans for use of the property. The courts have approved a five-year period for the removal of nonconforming billboards and a three-year period for the screening or removal of a nonconforming junkyard. Increasingly, restrictions on local government use of amortization have been proposed to and occasionally adopted by legislative bodies rather than the courts. For example, federal highway laws prevent the use of amortization to compel removal of billboards along federal highways.

Second, many zoning and subdivision ordinances require land developers to make dedications to the public as a condition of development approval. For example, there may be a requirement that streets and utilities be provided by the developer and turned over to the government. These requirements are legal so long as they are necessary to meet a legitimate governmental objective and so long as the size of the dedication is roughly proportional to the impacts of that development. For example, it is perfectly legitimate to require a developer to pave and dedicate to the public all internal streets within a new subdivision, to install utility lines to all lots being developed, or to contribute money to a park fund to build the recreation facilities needed by these new residents. But it would be impermissible to require the developer of a very small subdivision to build a major highway to serve the entire city, as a condition of government approval of the subdivision.

10 Statutory Limitations on Zoning Powers

For the most part, decisions about what land uses to regulate and how to do so are left to the discretion of local elected officials. However, since zoning is a power delegated from the state to local governments, the state can impose limits on zoning power in order to address statewide concerns. Federal legislation can also limit zoning powers.

State or federal governments can override local zoning decisions two ways. First, the state or federal government can decide to handle regulation of a certain topic by itself, thereby preempting any local regulation of that matter. For example, federal construction standards for manufactured homes override any state or local building code standards covering manufactured homes. This preemption can be explicitly stated in the law; alternatively, if a state or federal law completely addresses a subject, preemption is implied. The second way state or federal legislation controls local zoning is by mandating how the local regulation is to be carried out. For example, the state mandates that local zoning not completely exclude manufactured homes from an entire jurisdiction, but allows zoning ordinances to regulate the location, dimensions, and appearance of such homes.

This chapter discusses the state and federal limits imposed on local regulation of several particular land uses.

Agriculture. The North Carolina zoning enabling statutes exempt agricultural operations from coverage by county zoning. This exemption does not apply to zoning by cities, either within city boundaries or in a city's extraterritorial area.

Only bona fide farm operations are exempted. For the purposes of this exemption, farm operations include growing crops, raising livestock and poultry, and growing plants in a nursery. The exemption does not apply to commercial operations related to agriculture, such as a store selling fertilizer, a meat-packing operation, or a commercial grain-drying operation. Nor does it extend to nonfarm use of farms, such as placing a residence for a nonfarm worker on a farm.

Alcohol. The North Carolina courts have ruled that a state ABC permit overrides local zoning ordinances. When a person applies for an ABC permit to sell beer, wine, or mixed drinks, the permit application is circulated to local governments, who can comment as to whether the proposal is compatible with local zoning. The state will consider these comments, but is not required to follow them. If a permit is issued, the person can do what is allowed by the ABC permit even if it is inconsistent with zoning.

Some local governments attempt to impose restrictions on alcohol sales in permitted facilities. Examples include prohibiting a nonconforming restaurant in a residential district from selling alcohol or issuing a special-use permit that purports to limit the hours a convenience store can sell beer. Such restrictions are probably preempted by state regulations and are not enforceable through local zoning, though it will take further court cases to determine this.

Family-care homes. Family-care homes are facilities that provide health, counseling, or related services to a small number of persons in a family environment. Both state and federal laws affect zoning regulation of these facilities.

Under North Carolina law, a zoning ordinance must treat a family-care home the same as it treats any single-family residence. They cannot be prohibited in a district that allows single-family residences nor can they be subject to any special review requirements, such as a special- or conditional-use requirement. To qualify for this treatment, the facility must be designed to provide room, board, and care for six or fewer handicapped persons in a family environment. Handicapped persons include those with physical, emotional, or mental disabilities, but not those who have been deemed dangerous to themselves or to others. This state law does allow zoning ordinances to require a half-mile separation between family-care homes, but it is unclear if these minimum separations are valid under the Fair Housing Act.

In 1988 the federal Fair Housing Act was amended to prohibit local governments from discriminating against handicapped persons. This act makes it unlawful to prohibit or "otherwise make unavailable" housing for the handicapped. Local governments must also make "reasonable accommodation" for housing for the handicapped. For the purposes of this statute, "handicapped" includes any physical or mental impairment that limits a major life function, including disease and substance abuse. The exact scope of these prohibitions remains unclear and subject to ongoing litigation. For example, in a case involving a home for recovering alcoholics and drug addicts, the United States Supreme Court ruled that a zoning provision that limits the number of unrelated individuals who may occupy a house in a particular zoning district is subject to the Fair Housing Act. (Minimum housing codes that set a minimum square footage per individual resident *are* exempt.) So it is up to the local government to establish that a limit on the number of individuals residing in a house is neither unlawful discrimination nor a failure to make reasonable accommodation for handicapped persons. Requirements for minimum separations between family-care homes are also increasingly being challenged in court, with mixed results to date.

Historic districts and landmarks. Many zoning ordinances provide special coverage for historic neighborhoods and for particularly important individual historic structures. North Carolina has a special statute allowing protection of these resources through zoning and the state's courts have ruled that protection of these cultural and aesthetic resources is a valid exercise of zoning power.

Ordinances typically zone historic neighborhoods by placing them in a special zoning district, most often a *historic district overlay* that establishes special review requirements in addition to the basic zoning that already applies. The special restrictions require that a *certificate of appropriateness* be secured for any new construction, for any alteration of the exteriors of existing buildings, and for any demolition or removal of a structure. Similar protections can be established for individual buildings designated as historic landmarks. The standards for securing a certificate of appropriateness must be set out in the ordinance and must generally relate to maintenance of the particular character of that individual neighborhood. For example, a person would not be allowed to build a brick ranch in a neighborhood of Victorian homes or to build a Williamsburg-style home in a neighborhood of turn-of-the-century bungalows. These regulations can include a requirement stipulating that a permit to demolish a structure can be delayed for up to one year to allow time to develop a strategy for its preservation. The zoning ordinance commonly provides for a historic preservation commission to develop and administer these rules. Such a commission must have at least three members, and members must have set terms of up to four years and must reside within the jurisdiction. A majority of the members must have some special expertise in historic preservation. Another citizen board, such as the planning board or community appearance board, can serve as this commission if at least three of its members have the required special expertise. In addition to handling administrative responsibilities, these commissions can also acquire landmarks, restore and operate historic properties, and conduct educational programs.

Manufactured housing. In 1987 the state legislature directed North Carolina cities and counties to take steps to improve the supply of affordable housing. The legislation included provisions that zoning ordinances may not completely exclude *manufactured housing* (the current legal term for what used to be known as mobile homes or trailers) from an entire jurisdiction. Some zoning regulation of manufactured housing is allowed, however. Permissible restrictions include: (1) standards on location, such as allowing manufactured housing only in certain zoning districts or in mobile home parks; (2) dimensional requirements, such as allowing double-wide units only in certain zoning districts; and (3) appearance standards, such as requiring skirting be installed or requiring units to have pitched roofs.

These requirements apply only to units defined as *manufactured homes*, which are those built in a factory to federal construction standards (and having a HUD inspection sticker) rather than state building code standards. Some zoning ordinances apply similar standards to *modular homes*, which are factory built but are covered by the state building code rather than federal standards. Most ordinances, however, treat modular homes the same as conventional site-built housing.

Public buildings. In North Carolina the zoning enabling statutes provide that zoning ordinances apply to the erection, construction, and use of buildings by the state and its political subdivisions. Buildings used or constructed by state agencies, counties, cities, and utility districts must comply with zoning requirements. Governmental land uses that do not involve a building are not subject to local zoning. Buildings used by the federal government are not subject to local zoning. A post office, for example, can be located without regard to zoning, but the same is not true of a county jail or a city office building.

Satellite dishes. The federal government has placed limits on the extent to which local governments can regulate the location of satellite dishes. Satellite dishes are not exempt from zoning, but they do receive a degree of protection. Federal Communications Commission rules preempt any local zoning that differentiates between satellite dishes and other antennas unless there is a clearly defined health, safety, and aesthetic objective that does not impose unreasonable limitations or costs on the satellite dish owner. A historic district ordinance may preclude satellite dishes from the district if it also precludes other exterior antennas. A zoning restriction that limits satellite dishes to rear yards or requires some screening is generally permissible as long as this is not an undue burden in a particular situation.

Watersheds. One of the few places North Carolina mandates land-use regulation is in water supply watersheds. In 1989 the legislature mandated that those 200-plus local governments whose jurisdiction contains surface water bodies used for a public water supply adopt minimum land-use regulations to protect the quality of those waters. The primary aim of these regulations is to prevent harmful runoff into the water supplies, thus protecting public health and reducing the cost of water supply (it being cheaper to prevent contamination of the water than to clean it up). The state Environmental Management Commission classifies the state's watersheds, establishing the level of protection required; sets the minimum standards for local watershed ordinances; and reviews and approves each ordinance and any significant ordinance amendments.

These regulations limit certain uses, such as storage of hazardous materials or landfills near the water, and limit density of development that drains into these waters. The density limits for residential development take the form of minimum lot sizes; for commercial and industrial development, they put a limit on the amount of a lot that can be built on. The state rules do allow local governments to adopt a *high-density option* that permits more intensive development if the developer takes measures to control runoff, such as installing a pond to collect rainwater.

Appendix 1: Zoning Statutes

City Zoning Enabling Statutes

§ 160A-381. Grant of power.

For the purpose of promoting health, safety, morals, or the general welfare of the community, any city may regulate and restrict the height, number of stories and size of buildings and other structures, the percentage of lots that may be occupied, the size of yards, courts and other open spaces, the density of population, and the location and use of buildings, structures and land for trade, industry, residence or other purposes and to provide density credits or severable development rights for dedicated rights-of-way pursuant to G.S. 136-66.10 or G.S. 136-66.11. These regulations may provide that a board of adjustment may determine and vary their application in harmony with their general purpose and intent and in accordance with general or specific rules therein contained. The regulations may also provide that the board of adjustment or the city council may issue special use permits or conditional use permits in the classes of cases or situations and in accordance with the principles, conditions, safeguards, and procedures specified therein and may impose reasonable and appropriate conditions and safeguards upon these permits. Where appropriate, such conditions may include requirements that street and utility rights-of-way be dedicated to the public and that provision be made of recreational space and facilities. When issuing or denying special use permits or conditional use permits, the city council shall follow the procedures for boards of adjustment except that no vote greater than a majority vote shall be required for the city council to issue such permits, and every such decision of the city council shall be subject to review by the superior court by proceedings in the nature of certiorari. Any petition for review by the superior court shall be filed with the clerk of superior court within 30 days after the decision of the city council is filed in such office as the ordinance specifies, or after a written copy thereof is delivered to every aggrieved party who has filed a written request for such copy with the clerk at the time of the hearing of the case, whichever is later. The decision of the city council may be delivered to the aggrieved party either by personal service or by registered mail or certified mail return receipt requested.

§ 160A-382. Districts.

For any or all these purposes, the city may divide its territorial jurisdiction into districts of any number, shape, and area that may be deemed
best suited to carry out the purposes of this Part; and within those districts it may regulate and restrict the erection, construction, reconstruction, alteration, repair or use of buildings, structures, or land. Such districts may include, but shall not be limited to, general use districts, in
which a variety of uses are permissible in accordance with general standards; overlay districts, in which additional requirements are imposed on
certain properties within one or more underlying general or special use
districts; and special use districts or conditional use districts, in which
uses are permitted only upon the issuance of a special use permit or a
conditional use permit. Property may be placed in a special use district
or conditional use district only in response to a petition by the owners of
all the property to be included. Except as authorized by the foregoing, all
regulations shall be uniform for each class or kind of building throughout
each district, but the regulations in one district may differ from those in
other districts.

§ 160A-383. Purposes in view.

Zoning regulations shall be made in accordance with a comprehensive plan and designed to lessen congestion in the streets; to secure
safety from fire, panic and other dangers; to promote health and the general welfare; to provide adequate light and air; to prevent the overcrowding of land; to avoid undue concentration of population; and to facilitate
the adequate provision of transportation, water, sewerage, schools, parks,
and other public requirements. The regulations shall be made with reasonable consideration, among other things, as to the character of the district and its peculiar suitability for particular uses, and with a view to conserving the value of buildings and encouraging the most appropriate use
of land throughout such city.   .

§ 160A-383.1. Zoning regulations for manufactured homes.

(a) The General Assembly finds and declares that manufactured housing offers affordable housing opportunities for low and moderate income
residents of this State who could not otherwise afford to own their own
home. The General Assembly further finds that some local governments
have adopted zoning regulations which severely restrict the placement of
manufactured homes. It is the intent of the General Assembly in enacting
this section that cities reexamine their land use practices to assure compliance with applicable statutes and case law, and consider allocating

more residential land area for manufactured homes based upon local housing needs.

(b) For purposes of this section, the term "manufactured home" is defined as provided in G.S. 143-145(7).

(c) A city may not adopt or enforce zoning regulations or other provisions which have the effect of excluding manufactured homes from the entire zoning jurisdiction.

(d) A city may adopt and enforce appearance and dimensional criteria for manufactured homes. Such criteria shall be designed to protect property values, to preserve the character and integrity of the community or individual neighborhoods within the community, and to promote the health, safety and welfare of area residents. The criteria shall be adopted by ordinance.

(e) In accordance with the city's comprehensive plan and based on local housing needs, a city may designate a manufactured home overlay district within a residential district. Such overlay district may not consist of an individual lot or scattered lots, but shall consist of a defined area within which additional requirements or standards are placed upon manufactured homes.

(f) Nothing in this section shall be construed to preempt or supersede valid restrictive covenants running with the land. The terms "mobile home" and "trailer" in any valid restrictive covenants running with the land shall include the term "manufactured home" as defined in this section.

§ 160A-384. Method of procedure.

(a) The city council shall provide for the manner in which zoning regulations and restrictions and the boundaries of zoning districts shall be determined, established and enforced, and from time to time amended, supplemented or changed, in accordance with the provisions of this Article. The procedures adopted pursuant to this section shall provide that whenever there is a zoning map amendment, the owner of that parcel of land as shown on the county tax listing, and the owners of all parcels of land abutting that parcel of land as shown on the county tax listing, shall be mailed a notice of a public hearing on the proposed amendment by first class mail at the last addresses listed for such owners on the county tax abstracts. This notice must be deposited in the mail at least 10 but not more than 25 days prior to the date of the public hearing. The person or persons mailing such notices shall certify to the City Council that fact, and such certificate shall be deemed conclusive in the absence of fraud.

(b) The first class mail notice required under subsection (a) of this section shall not be required if the zoning map amendment directly affects more than 50 properties, owned by a total of at least 50 different property owners, and the city elects to use the expanded published notice provided for in this subsection. In this instance, a city may elect to either make the mailed notice provided for in subsection (a) of this section or may as an alternative elect to publish once a week for four successive calendar weeks in a newspaper having general circulation in the area an advertisement of the public hearing that shows the boundaries of the area affected by the proposed zoning map amendment and explains the nature of the proposed change. The final two advertisements shall comply with and be deemed to satisfy the provisions of G.S. 160A-364. The advertisement shall not be less than one-half of a newspaper page in size. The advertisement shall only be effective for property owners who reside in the area of general circulation of the newspaper which publishes the notice. Property owners who reside outside of the newspaper circulation area, according to the address listed on the most recent property tax listing for the affected property, shall be notified by first class mail pursuant to this section. The person or persons mailing the notices shall certify to the city council that fact, and the certificates shall be deemed conclusive in the absence of fraud. In addition to the published notice, a city shall post one or more prominent signs on or immediately adjacent to the subject area reasonably calculated to give public notice of the proposed rezoning.

§ 160A-385. Changes.

(a) Zoning regulations and restrictions and zone boundaries may from time to time be amended, supplemented, changed, modified or repealed. In case, however, of a protest against such change, signed by the owners of twenty percent (20%) or more either of the area of the lots included in a proposed change, or of those immediately adjacent thereto either in the rear thereof or on either side thereof, extending 100 feet therefrom, or of those directly opposite thereto extending 100 feet from the street frontage of the opposite lots, an amendment shall not become effective except by favorable vote of three-fourths of all the members of the city council. The foregoing provisions concerning protests shall not be applicable to any amendment which initially zones property added to the territorial coverage of the ordinance as a result of annexation or otherwise, or to an amendment to an adopted special use district or conditional use district if the amendment does not change the types of uses that are permitted within the district or increase the approved density for residential development, or increase the total approved size of nonresidential development, or reduce the size of any buffers or screening approved for the special use or conditional use district.

(b) Amendments, modifications, supplements, repeal or other changes in zoning regulations and restrictions and zone boundaries shall not be applicable or enforceable without consent of the owner with regard to buildings and uses for which either (i) building permits have been issued pursuant to G.S. 160A-417 prior to the enactment of the ordinance making the change or changes so long as the permits remain valid and unexpired pursuant to G.S. 160A-418 and unrevoked pursuant to G.S. 160A-422 or (ii) a vested right has been established pursuant to G.S. 160A-385.1 and such vested right remains valid and unexpired pursuant to G.S. 160A-385.1.

§ 160A-385.1. Vested rights.

(a) The General Assembly finds and declares that it is necessary and desirable, as a matter of public policy, to provide for the establishment of certain vested rights in order to ensure reasonable certainty, stability, and fairness in the land-use planning process, secure the reasonable expectations of landowners, and foster cooperation between the public and private sectors in the area of land-use planning. Furthermore, the General Assembly recognizes that city approval of land-use development typically follows significant landowner investment in site evaluation, planning, development costs, consultant fees, and related expenses.

The ability of a landowner to obtain a vested right after city approval of a site specific development plan or a phased development plan will preserve the prerogatives and authority of local elected officials with respect to land-use matters. There will be ample opportunities for public participation and the public interest will be served. These provisions will strike an appropriate balance between private expectations and the public interest, while scrupulously protecting the public health, safety, and welfare.

(b) Definitions.

(1) "Landowner" means any owner of a legal or equitable interest in real property, including the heirs, devisees, successors, assigns, and personal representative of such owner. The landowner may allow a person holding a valid option to purchase to act as his agent or representative for purposes of submitting a proposed site specific development plan or a phased development plan under this section, in the manner allowed by ordinance.

(2) "City" shall have the same meaning as set forth in G.S. 160A-1(2).

(3) "Phased development plan" means a plan which has been submitted to a city by a landowner for phased development which shows the type and intensity of use for a specific parcel or parcels with a lesser degree of certainty than the plan determined by the city to be a site specific development plan.

(4) "Property" means all real property subject to zoning regulations and restrictions and zone boundaries by a city.

(5) "Site specific development plan" means a plan which has been submitted to a city by a landowner describing with reasonable certainty

the type and intensity of use for a specific parcel or parcels of property. Such plan may be in the form of, but not be limited to, any of the following plans or approvals: A planned unit development plan, a subdivision plat, a preliminary or general development plan, a conditional or special use permit, a conditional or special use district zoning plan, or any other land-use approval designation as may be utilized by a city. Unless otherwise expressly provided by the city, such a plan shall include the approximate boundaries of the site; significant topographical and other natural features effecting development of the site; the approximate location on the site of the proposed buildings, structures, and other improvements; the approximate dimensions, including height, of the proposed buildings and other structures; and the approximate location of all existing and proposed infrastructure on the site, including water, sewer, roads, and pedestrian walkways. What constitutes a site specific development plan under this section that would trigger a vested right shall be finally determined by the city pursuant to an ordinance, and the document that triggers such vesting shall be so identified at the time of its approval. However, at a minimum, the ordinance to be adopted by the city shall designate a vesting point earlier than the issuance of a building permit. A variance shall not constitute a site specific development plan, and approval of a site specific development plan with the condition that a variance be obtained shall not confer a vested right unless and until the necessary variance is obtained. Neither a sketch plan nor any other document which fails to describe with reasonable certainty the type and intensity of use for a specified parcel or parcels of property may constitute a site specific development plan.

(6) "Vested right" means the right to undertake and complete the development and use of property under the terms and conditions of an approved site specific development plan or an approved phased development plan.

(c) Establishment of vested right.

A vested right shall be deemed established with respect to any property upon the valid approval, or conditional approval, of a site specific development plan or a phased development plan, following notice and public hearing by the city with jurisdiction over the property. Such vested right shall confer upon the landowner the right to undertake and complete the development and use of said property under the terms and conditions of the site specific development plan or the phased development plan including any amendments thereto. A city may approve a site specific development plan or a phased development plan upon such terms and conditions as may reasonably be necessary to protect the public health, safety, and welfare. Such conditional approval shall result in a vested right, although failure to abide by such terms and conditions will result in a forfeiture of vested rights. A city shall not require a landowner to waive his vested rights as a condition of developmental approval. A site specific development plan or a phase development plan shall be deemed approved upon the effective date of the city's action or ordinance relating thereto.

(d) Duration and termination of vested right.

(1) A right which has been vested as provided for in this section shall remain vested for a period of two years. This vesting shall not be extended by any amendments or modifications to a site specific development plan unless expressly provided by the city.

(2) Notwithstanding the provisions of subsection (d)(1), a city may provide that rights shall be vested for a period exceeding two years but not exceeding five years where warranted in light of all relevant circumstances, including, but not limited to, the size and phasing of development, the level of investment, the need for the development, economic cycles, and market conditions. These determinations shall be in the sound discretion of the city.

(3) Notwithstanding the provisions of (d)(1) and (d)(2), the city may provide by ordinance that approval by a city of a phased development plan shall vest the zoning classification or classifications so approved for a period not to exceed five years. The document that triggers such vesting shall be so identified at the time of its approval. The city still may require the landowner to submit a site specific development plan for approval by the city with respect to each phase or phases in order to obtain final approval to develop within the restrictions of the vested zoning classification or classifications. Nothing in this section shall be construed to require a city to adopt an ordinance providing for vesting of rights upon approval of a phased development plan.

(4) Following approval or conditional approval of a site specific development plan or a phased development plan, nothing in this section shall exempt such a plan from subsequent reviews and approvals by the city to ensure compliance with the terms and conditions of the original approval, provided that such reviews and approvals are not inconsistent with said original approval. Nothing in this section shall prohibit the city from revoking the original approval for failure to comply with applicable terms and conditions of the approval or the zoning ordinance.

(5) Upon issuance of a building permit, the provisions of G.S. 160A-418 and G.S. 160A-422 shall apply, except that a permit shall not expire or be revoked because of the running of time while a vested right under this section is outstanding.

(6) A right which has been vested as provided in this section shall terminate at the end of the applicable vesting period with respect to buildings and uses for which no valid building permit applications have been filed.

(e) Subsequent changes prohibited; exceptions.

(1) A vested right, once established as provided for in this section, precludes any zoning action by a city which would change, alter, impair, prevent, diminish, or otherwise delay the development or use of the property as set forth in an approved site specific development plan or an approved phased development plan, except:

a. With the written consent of the affected landowner;

b. Upon findings, by ordinance after notice and a public hearing, that natural or man-made hazards on or in the immediate vicinity of the property, if uncorrected, would pose a serious threat to the public health, safety, and welfare if the project were to proceed as contemplated in the site specific development plan or the phased development plan;

c. To the extent that the affected landowner receives compensation for all costs, expenses, and other losses incurred by the landowner, including, but not limited to, all fees paid in consideration of financing, and all architectural, planning, marketing, legal, and other consultant's fees incurred after approval by the city, together with interest thereon at the legal rate until paid. Compensation shall not include any diminution in the value of the property which is caused by such action;

d. Upon findings, by ordinance after notice and a hearing, that the landowner or his representative intentionally supplied inaccurate information or made material misrepresentations which made a difference in the approval by the city of the site specific development plan or the phased development plan; or

e. Upon the enactment or promulgation of a State or federal law or regulation which precludes development as contemplated in the site specific development plan or the phased development plan, in which case the city may modify the affected provisions, upon a finding that the change in State or federal law has a fundamental effect on the plan, by ordinance after notice and a hearing.

(2) The establishment of a vested right shall not preclude the application of overlay zoning which imposes additional requirements but does not affect the allowable type or intensity of use, or ordinances or regulations which are general in nature and are applicable to all property subject to land-use regulation by a city, including, but not limited to, building, fire, plumbing, electrical, and mechanical codes. Otherwise applicable new regulations shall become effective with respect to property which is subject to a site specific development plan or a phased development plan upon the expiration or termination of the vesting rights period provided for in this section.

(3) Notwithstanding any provision of this section, the establishment of a vested right shall not preclude, change or impair the authority of a city to adopt and enforce zoning ordinance provisions governing nonconforming situations or uses.

(f) Miscellaneous provisions.

(1) A vested right obtained under this section is not a personal right, but shall attach to and run with the applicable property. After approval of a site specific development plan or a phased development plan, all successors to the original landowner shall be entitled to exercise such rights.

(2) Nothing in this section shall preclude judicial determination, based on common law principles or other statutory provisions, that a vested right exists in a particular case or that a compensable taking has occurred. Except as expressly provided in this section, nothing in this section shall be construed to alter the existing common law.

(3) In the event a city fails to adopt an ordinance setting forth what constitutes a site specific development plan triggering a vested right, a landowner may establish a vested right with respect to property upon the approval of a zoning permit, or otherwise may seek appropriate relief from the Superior Court Division of the General Court of Justice.

§ 160A-386. Protest petition; form; requirements; time for filing.

No protest against any change in or amendment to a zoning ordinance or zoning map shall be valid or effective for the purposes of G.S. 160A-385 unless it be in the form of a written petition actually bearing the signatures of the requisite number of property owners and stating that the signers do protest the proposed change or amendment, and unless it shall have been received by the city clerk in sufficient time to allow the city at least two normal work days, excluding Saturdays, Sundays and legal holidays, before the date established for a public hearing on the proposed change or amendment to determine the sufficiency and accuracy of the petition. The city council may by ordinance require that all protest petitions be on a form prescribed and furnished by the city, and such form may prescribe any reasonable information deemed necessary to permit the city to determine the sufficiency and accuracy of the petition.

§ 160A-387. Planning agency; zoning plan; certification to city council.

In order to exercise the powers conferred by this Part, a city council shall create or designate a planning agency under the provisions of this Article or of a special act of the General Assembly. The planning agency shall prepare a proposed zoning ordinance, including both the full text of such ordinance and maps showing proposed district boundaries. The planning agency may hold public hearings in the course of preparing the ordinance. Upon completion, the planning agency shall certify the ordinance to the city council. The city council shall not hold its required public hearing or take action until it has received a certified ordinance from the planning agency. Following its required public hearing, the city council may refer the ordinance back to the planning agency for any further recommendations that the agency may wish to make prior to final action by the city council in adopting, modifying and adopting, or rejecting the ordinance.

§ 160A-388. Board of adjustment.

(a) The city council may provide for the appointment and compensation of a board of adjustment consisting of five or more members, each to be appointed for three years. In appointing the original members of such board, or in the filling of vacancies caused by the expiration of the terms of existing members, the council may appoint certain members for less than three years to the end that thereafter the terms of all members shall not expire at the same time. The council may, in its discretion, appoint and provide compensation for alternate members to serve on the board in the absence of any regular member. Alternate members shall be appointed for the same term, at the same time, and in the same manner as regular members. Each alternate member, while attending any regular or special meeting of the board and serving in the absence of any regular member, shall have and may exercise all the powers and duties of a regular member. A city may designate a planning agency to perform any or all of the duties of a board of adjustment in addition to its other duties.

(b) The board of adjustment shall hear and decide appeals from and review any order, requirement, decision, or determination made by an administrative official charged with the enforcement of any ordinance adopted pursuant to this Part. An appeal may be taken by any person aggrieved or by an officer, department, board, or bureau of the city. Appeals shall be taken within times prescribed by the board of adjustment by general rule, by filing with the officer from whom the appeal is taken and with the board of adjustment a notice of appeal, specifying the grounds thereof. The officer from whom the appeal is taken shall forthwith transmit to the board all the papers constituting the record upon which the action appealed from was taken. An appeal stays all proceedings in furtherance of the action appealed from, unless the officer from whom the appeal is taken certifies to the board of adjustment, after notice of appeal has been filed with him, that because of facts stated in the certificate a stay would, in his opinion, cause imminent peril to life or property or that because the violation charged is transitory in nature a stay would seriously interfere with enforcement of the ordinance. In that case proceedings shall not be stayed except by a restraining order, which may be granted by the board of adjustment or by a court of record on application, on notice to the officer from whom the appeal is taken and on due cause shown. The board of adjustment shall fix a reasonable time for the hearing of the appeal, give due notice thereof to the parties, and decide it within a reasonable time. The board of adjustment may reverse or affirm, wholly or partly, or may modify the order, requirement, decision, or determination appealed from, and shall make any order, requirement, decision, or determination that in its opinion ought to be made in the premises. To this end the board shall have all the powers of the officer from whom the appeal is taken.

(c) The zoning ordinance may provide that the board of adjustment may permit special exceptions to the zoning regulations in classes of cases or situations and in accordance with the principles, conditions, safeguards, and procedures specified in the ordinance. The ordinance may also authorize the board to interpret zoning maps and pass upon disputed questions of lot lines or district boundary lines and similar questions as they arise in the administration of the ordinance. The board shall hear and decide all matters referred to it or upon which it is required to pass under any zoning ordinance.

(d) When practical difficulties or unnecessary hardships would result from carrying out the strict letter of a zoning ordinance, the board of adjustment shall have the power, in passing upon appeals, to vary or modify any of the regulations or provisions of the ordinance relating to the use, construction or alteration of buildings or structures or the use of land, so that the spirit of the ordinance shall be observed, public safety and welfare secured, and substantial justice done.

(e) The concurring vote of four-fifths of the members of the board shall be necessary to reverse any order, requirement, decision, or determination of any administrative official charged with the enforcement of an ordinance adopted pursuant to this Part, or to decide in favor of the applicant any matter upon which it is required to pass under any ordinance, or to grant a variance from the provisions of the ordinance. Every decision of the board shall be subject to review by the superior court by proceedings in the nature of certiorari. Any petition for review by the superior court shall be filed with the clerk of superior court within 30 days after the decision of the board is filed in such office as the ordinance specifies, or after a written copy thereof is delivered to every aggrieved party who has filed a written request for such copy with the secretary or chairman of the board at the time of its hearing of the case, whichever is later. The decision of the board may be delivered to the aggrieved party either by personal service or by registered mail or certified mail return receipt requested.

(f) The chairman of the board of adjustment or any member temporarily acting as chairman, is authorized in his official capacity to administer oaths to witnesses in any matter coming before the board.

(g) The board of adjustment may subpoena witnesses and compel the production of evidence. If a person fails or refuses to obey a subpoena issued pursuant to this subsection, the board of adjustment may apply to the General Court of Justice for an order requiring that its order be obeyed, and the court shall have jurisdiction to issue these orders after notice to all proper parties. No testimony of any witness before the board of adjustment pursuant to a subpoena issued in exercise of the power conferred by this subsection may be used against the witness in the trial of any civil or criminal action other than a prosecution for false swearing committed on the examination. Any person who, while under oath during a proceeding before the board of adjustment, willfully swears falsely, is guilty of a Class 1 misdemeanor.

§ 160A-389. Remedies.

If a building or structure is erected, constructed, reconstructed, altered, repaired, converted, or maintained, or any building, structure or land is used in violation of this Part or of any ordinance or other regulation made under authority conferred thereby, the city, in addition to other remedies, may institute any appropriate action or proceedings to prevent the unlawful erection, construction, reconstruction, alteration, repair, conversion, maintenance or use, to restrain, correct or abate the violation, to prevent occupancy of the building, structure or land, or to prevent any illegal act, conduct, business or use in or about the premises.

§ 160A-390. Conflict with other laws.

When regulations made under authority of this Part require a greater width or size of yards or courts, or require a lower height of a building or fewer number of stories, or require a greater percentage of a lot to be left unoccupied, or impose other higher standards than are required in any other statute or local ordinance or regulation, regulations made under authority of this Part shall govern. When the provisions of any other statute or local ordinance or regulation require a greater width or size of yards or courts, or require a lower height of a building or a fewer number of stories, or require a greater percentage of a lot to be left unoccupied, or impose other higher standards than are required by the regulations made under authority of this Part, the provisions of that statute or local ordinance or regulation shall govern.

§ 160A-391. Other statutes not repealed.

This Part shall not repeal any zoning act or city planning act, local or general, now in force, except those that are repugnant to or inconsistent herewith. This Part shall be construed to be an enlargement of the duties, powers, and authority contained in other laws authorizing the appointment and proper functioning of city planning commissions or zoning commissions by any city or town in the State of North Carolina.

§ 160A-392. Part applicable to buildings constructed by State and its subdivisions; exception.

All of the provisions of this Part are hereby made applicable to the erection, construction, and use of buildings by the State of North Carolina and its political subdivisions.

Notwithstanding the provisions of any general or local law or ordinance, no land owned by the State of North Carolina may be included within an overlay district or a special use or conditional use district without approval of the Council of State.

County Zoning Enabling Statutes

§ 153A-340. Grant of power.

For the purpose of promoting health, safety, morals, or the general welfare, a county may regulate and restrict the height, number of stories and size of buildings and other structures, the percentage of lots that may be occupied, the size of yards, courts and other open spaces, the density of population, and the location and use of buildings, structures, and land for trade, industry, residence, or other purposes, and to provide density credits or severable development rights for dedicated rights-of-way pursuant to G.S. 136-66.10 or G.S. 136-66.11.

These regulations may not affect bona fide farms, but any use of farm property for nonfarm purposes is subject to the regulations. Bona fide farm purposes include the production and activities relating or incidental to the production of crops, fruits, vegetables, ornamental and flowering plants, dairy, livestock, poultry, and all other forms of agricultural products having a domestic or foreign market. The regulations may provide that a board of adjustment may determine and vary their application in harmony with their general purpose and intent and in accordance with general or specific rules therein contained. The regulations may also provide that the board of adjustment or the board of commissioners may issue special use permits or conditional use permits in the classes of cases or situations and in accordance with the principles, conditions, safeguards, and procedures specified therein and may impose reasonable and appropriate conditions and safeguards upon these permits. Where appropriate, the conditions may include requirements that street and utility rights-of-way be dedicated to the public and that recreational space be provided. When issuing or denying special use permits or conditional use permits, the board of commissioners shall follow the procedures for boards of adjustment except that no vote greater than a majority vote shall be required for the board of commissioners to issue such permits, and every such decision of the board of commissioners shall be subject to review by the superior court by proceedings in the nature of certiorari.

A county may regulate the development over estuarine waters and over lands covered by navigable waters owned by the State pursuant to G.S. 146-12, within the bounds of that county.

For the purpose of this section, the term "structures" shall include floating homes. Any petition for review by the superior court shall be filed with the clerk of superior court within 30 days after the decision of the board of commissioners is filed in such office as the ordinance specifies, or after a written copy thereof is delivered to every aggrieved party who has filed a written request for such copy with the clerk at the time of the hearing of the case, whichever is later. The decision of the board of commissioners may be delivered to the aggrieved party either by personal service or by registered mail or certified mail return receipt requested.

§ 153A-341. Purposes in view.

Zoning regulations shall be made in accordance with a comprehensive plan and designed to lessen congestion in the streets; to secure safety from fire, panic, and other dangers; to promote health and the general welfare; to provide adequate light and air; to prevent the overcrowding of land; to avoid undue concentration of population; and to facilitate the adequate provision of transportation, water, sewerage, schools, parks, and other public requirements. The regulations shall be made with reasonable consideration as to, among other things, the character of the district and its peculiar suitability for particular uses, and with a view to conserving the value of buildings and encouraging the most appropriate use of land throughout the county. In addition, the regulations shall be made with reasonable consideration to expansion and development of any cities within the county, so as to provide for their orderly growth and development. ·

§ 153A-341.1. Zoning regulations for manufactured homes.

The provisions of G.S. 160A-383.1 shall apply to counties.

§ 153A-342. Districts; zoning less than entire jurisdiction.

A county may divide its territorial jurisdiction into districts of any number, shape, and area that it may consider best suited to carry out the purposes of this Part. Within these districts a county may regulate and restrict the erection, construction, reconstruction, alteration, repair, or use of buildings, structures, or land. Such districts may include, but shall not be limited to, general use districts, in which a variety of uses are permissible in accordance with general standards; overlay districts, in which additional requirements are imposed on certain properties within one or more underlying general or special use districts; and special use districts or conditional use districts, in which uses are permitted only upon the issuance of a special use permit or a conditional use permit. Property may be placed in a special use district or conditional use district only in response to a petition by the owners of all the property to be included. Except as authorized by the foregoing, all regulations shall be uniform for each class or kind of building throughout each district, but the regulations in one district may differ from those in other districts.

A county may determine that the public interest does not require that the entire territorial jurisdiction of the county be zoned and may designate one or more portions of that jurisdiction as a zoning area or areas. A zoning area must originally contain at least 640 acres and at least 10 separate tracts of land in separate ownership and may thereafter be expanded by the addition of any amount of territory. A zoning area may be regulated in the same manner as if the entire county were zoned, and the remainder of the county need not be regulated.

§ 153A-343. Method of procedure.

(a) The board of commissioners shall, in accordance with the provisions of this Article, provide for the manner in which zoning regulations and restrictions and the boundaries of zoning districts shall be determined, established, and enforced, and from time to time amended, supplemented, or changed. The procedures adopted pursuant to this section shall provide that whenever there is a zoning map amendment, the owner of that parcel of land as shown on the county tax listing, and the owners of all parcels of land abutting that parcel of land as shown on the county tax listing, shall be mailed a notice of a public hearing on the proposed amendment by first class mail at the last addresses listed for such owners on the county tax abstracts. This notice must be deposited in the mail at least 10 but not more than 25 days prior to the date of the public hearing. The person or persons mailing such notices shall certify to the Board of Commissioners that fact, and such certificate shall be deemed conclusive in the absence of fraud.

(b) The first class mail notice required under subsection (a) of this section shall not be required if the zoning map amendment directly affects more than 50 properties, owned by a total of at least 50 different property owners, and the county elects to use the expanded published notice provided for in this subsection. In this instance, a county may elect to either make the mailed notice provided for in subsection (a) of this section or may as an alternative elect to publish once a week for four successive calendar weeks in a newspaper having general circulation in the area an advertisement of the public hearing that shows the boundaries of the area affected by the proposed zoning map and explains the nature of the proposed change. The final two advertisements shall comply with and be deemed to satisfy the provisions of G.S. 153A-323. The advertisement shall not be less than one-half of a newspaper page in size. The advertisement shall only be effective for property owners who reside in the area of general circulation of the newspaper which publishes the notice. Property owners who reside outside of the newspaper circulation area, according to the address listed on the most recent property tax listing for the affected property, shall be notified by first class mail pursuant to this section. The person or persons mailing the notices shall certify to the board of commissioners that fact, and the certificates shall be deemed conclusive in the absence of fraud. In addition to the published notice, a county shall post one or more prominent signs on or immediately adjacent to the subject area reasonably calculated to give public notice of the proposed rezoning.

(c) The provisions of this section shall not be applicable to any zoning map adoption that initially zones property added to the territorial coverage of the ordinance.

§ 153A-344. Planning agency; zoning plan; certification to board of commissioners; amendments.

(a) To exercise the powers conferred by this Part, a county shall create or designate a planning agency under the provisions of this Article or of a local act. The planning agency shall prepare a proposed zoning ordinance, including both the full text of such ordinance and maps showing proposed district boundaries. The planning agency may hold public hearings in the course of preparing the ordinance. Upon completion, the planning agency shall certify the ordinance to the board of commissioners. The board of commissioners shall not hold the public hearing required by G.S. 153A-323 or take action until it has received a certified ordinance from the planning agency. Following its required public hearing, the board of commissioners may refer the ordinance back to the planning agency for any further recommendations that the agency may wish to make prior to final action by the board in adopting, modifying and adopting, or rejecting the ordinance.

Zoning regulations and restrictions and zone boundaries may from time to time be amended, supplemented, changed, modified, or repealed. Whenever territory is added to an existing designated zoning area, it shall be treated as an amendment to the zoning ordinance for that area. Before an amendment may be adopted, it must be referred to the planning agency for the agency's recommendation. The agency shall be given at least 30 days in which to make a recommendation. The board of commissioners is not bound by the recommendations, if any, of the planning agency.

(b) Amendments, modifications, supplements, repeal or other changes in zoning regulations and restrictions and zone boundaries shall not be applicable or enforceable without consent of the owner with regard to buildings and uses for which either (i) building permits have been issued pursuant to G.S. 153A-357 prior to the enactment of the ordinance making the change or changes so long as the permits remain valid and unexpired pursuant to G.S. 153A-358 and unrevoked pursuant to G.S. 153A-362 or (ii) a vested right has been established pursuant to G.S. 153A-344.1 and such vested right remains valid and unexpired pursuant to G.S. 153A-344.1.

§ 153A-344.1. Vesting rights.

(a) The General Assembly finds and declares that it is necessary and desirable, as a matter of public policy, to provide for the establishment of certain vested rights in order to ensure reasonable certainty, stability, and fairness in the land-use planning process, secure the reasonable expectations of landowners, and foster cooperation between the public and private sectors in the area of land-use planning. Furthermore, the General Assembly recognizes that county approval of land-use development typically follows significant landowner investment in site evaluation, planning, development costs, consultant fees, and related expenses.

The ability of a landowner to obtain a vested right after county approval of a site specific development plan or a phased development plan will preserve the prerogatives and authority of local elected officials with respect to land-use matters. There will be ample opportunities for public participation and the public interest will be served. These provisions will strike an appropriate balance between private expectations and the public interest, while scrupulously protecting the public health, safety, and welfare.

(b) Definitions.

(1) "Landowner" means any owner of a legal or equitable interest in real property, including the heirs, devisees, successors, assigns, and personal representative of such owner. The landowner may allow a person holding a valid option to purchase to act as his agent or representative for purposes of submitting a proposed site specific development plan or a phased development plan under this section, in the manner allowed by ordinance.

(2) "County" shall have the same meaning as set forth in G.S. 153A-1 (3).

(3) "Phased development plan" means a plan which has been submitted to a county by a landowner for phased development which shows the type and intensity of use for a specific parcel or parcels with a lesser degree of certainty than the plan determined by the county to be a site specific development plan.

(4) "Property" means all real property subject to zoning regulations and restrictions and zone boundaries by a county.

(5) "Site specific development plan" means a plan which has been submitted to a county by a landowner describing with reasonable certainty the type and intensity of use for a specific parcel or parcels of property. Such plan may be in the form of, but not be limited to, any of the following plans or approvals: A planned unit development plan, a subdivision plat, a preliminary or general development plan, a conditional or special use permit, a conditional or special use district zoning plan, or any other land-use approval designation as may be utilized by a county. Unless otherwise expressly provided by the county such a plan shall include the approximate boundaries of the site; significant topographical and other natural features effecting development of the site; the approximate location on the site of the proposed buildings, structures, and other improvements; the approximate dimensions, including height, of the proposed buildings and other structures; and the approximate location of all existing and proposed infrastructure on the site, including water, sewer, roads, and pedestrian walkways. What constitutes a site specific development plan under this section that would trigger a vested right shall be finally determined by the county pursuant to an ordinance, and the document that triggers such vesting shall be so identified at the time of its approval. However, at a minimum, the ordinance to be adopted by the county shall designate a vesting point earlier than the issuance of a building permit. A variance shall not constitute a site specific development plan, and approval of a site specific development plan with the condition that a variance be obtained shall not confer a vested right unless and until the necessary variance is obtained. Neither a sketch plan nor any other document which fails to describe with reasonable certainty the type and intensity of use for a specified parcel or parcels or property may constitute a site specific development plan.

(6) "Vested right" means the right to undertake and complete the development and use of property under the terms and conditions of an approved site specific development plan or an approved phased development plan.

(c) Establishment of vested right.

A vested right shall be deemed established with respect to any property upon the valid approval, or conditional approval, of a site specific development plan or a phased development plan, following notice and public hearing by the county with jurisdiction over the property. Such vested right shall confer upon the landowner the right to undertake and complete the development and use of said property under the terms and conditions of the site specific development plan or the phased development plan including any amendments thereto. A county may approve a site specific development plan or a phased development plan upon such terms and conditions as may reasonably be necessary to protect the public health, safety, and welfare. Such conditional approval shall result in a vested right, although failure to abide by such terms and conditions will result in a forfeiture of vested rights. A county shall not require a landowner to waive his vested rights as a condition of developmental approval. A site specific development plan or a phased development plan shall be deemed approved upon the effective date of the county's action or ordinance relating thereto.

(d) Duration and termination of vested right.

(1) A right which has been vested as provided for in this section shall remain vested for a period of two years. This vesting shall not be extended by any amendments or modifications to a site specific development plan unless expressly provided by the county.

(2) Notwithstanding the provisions of subsection (d)(1), a county may provide that rights shall be vested for a period exceeding two years but not exceeding five years where warranted in light of all relevant circumstances, including, but not limited to, the size and phasing of development, the level of investment, the need for the development, economic cycles, and market conditions. These determinations shall be in the sound discretion of the county.

(3) Notwithstanding the provisions of (d)(1) and (d)(2), the county may provide by ordinance that approval by a county of a phased development plan shall vest the zoning classification or classifications so approved for a period not to exceed five years. The document that triggers such vesting shall be so identified at the time of its approval. The county still may require the landowner to submit a site specific development plan for approval by the county with respect to each phase or phases in order to obtain final approval to develop within the restrictions of the vested zoning classification or classifications. Nothing in this section shall be construed to require a county to adopt an ordinance providing for vesting of rights upon approval of a phased development plan.

(4) Following approval or conditional approval of a site specific development plan or a phased development plan, nothing in this section shall exempt such a plan from subsequent reviews and approvals by the county to ensure compliance with the terms and conditions of the original approval, provided that such reviews and approvals are not inconsistent with said original approval. Nothing in this section shall prohibit the county from revoking the original approval for failure to comply with applicable terms and conditions of the approval or the zoning ordinance.

(5) Upon issuance of a building permit, the provisions of G.S. 153A-358 and G.S. 153A-362 shall apply, except that a permit shall not expire or be revoked because of the running of time while a vested right under this section is outstanding.

(6) A right which has been vested as provided in this section shall terminate at the end of the applicable vesting period with respect to buildings and uses for which no valid building permit applications have been filed.

(e) Subsequent changes prohibited; exceptions.

(1) A vested right, once established as provided for in this section, precludes any zoning action by a county which would change, alter, impair, prevent, diminish, or otherwise delay the development or use of the property as set forth in an approved site specific development plan or an approved phased development plan, except:

a. With the written consent of the affected landowner;

b. Upon findings, by ordinance after notice and a public hearing, that natural or man-made hazards on or in the immediate vicinity of the property, if uncorrected, would pose a serious threat to the public health, safety, and welfare if the project were to proceed as contemplated in the site specific development plan or the phased development plan;

c. To the extent that the affected landowner receives compensation for all costs, expenses, and other losses incurred by the landowner, including, but not limited to, all fees paid in consideration of financing, and all architectural, planning, marketing, legal, and other consultant's fees incurred after approval by the county, together with interest thereon at the legal rate until paid. Compensation shall not include any diminution in the value of the property which is caused by such action;

d. Upon findings, by ordinance after notice and a hearing, that the landowner or his representative intentionally supplied inaccurate information or made material misrepresentations which made a difference in the approval by the county of the site specific development plan or the phased development plan; or

e. Upon the enactment or promulgation of a State or federal law or regulation which precludes development as contemplated in the site specific development plan or the phased development plan, in which case the county may modify the affected provisions, upon a finding that the change in State or federal law has a fundamental effect on the plan, by ordinance after notice and a hearing.

(2) The establishment of a vested right shall not preclude the application of overlay zoning which imposes additional requirements but does not affect the allowable type or intensity of use, or ordinances or regulations which are general in nature and are applicable to all property subject to land-use regulation by a county, including, but not limited to, building, fire, plumbing, electrical, and mechanical codes. Otherwise applicable new regulations shall become effective with respect to property which is subject to a site specific development plan or a phased development plan upon the expiration or termination of the vesting rights period provided for in this section.

(3) Notwithstanding any provision of this section, the establishment of a vested right shall not preclude, change or impair the authority of a county to adopt and enforce zoning ordinance provisions governing nonconforming situations or uses.

(f) Miscellaneous provisions.

(1) A vested right obtained under this section is not a personal right, but shall attach to and run with the applicable property. After approval of a site specific development plan or a phased development plan, all successors to the original landowner shall be entitled to exercise such rights.

(2) Nothing in this section shall preclude judicial determination, based on common-law principles or other statutory provisions, that a vested right exists in a particular case or that a compensable taking has occurred. Except as expressly provided in this section, nothing in this section shall be construed to alter the existing common law.

(3) In the event a county fails to adopt an ordinance setting forth what constitutes a site specific development plan triggering a vested right, a landowner may establish a vested right with respect to property upon the approval of a zoning permit, or otherwise may seek appropriate relief from the Superior Court Division of the General Court of Justice.

§ 153A-345. Board of adjustment.

(a) The board of commissioners may provide for the appointment and compensation, if any, of a board of adjustment consisting of at least five members, each to be appointed for three years. In appointing the original members of the board, or in filling vacancies caused by the expiration of the terms of existing members, the board of commissioners may appoint some members for less than three years to the end that thereafter the terms of all members do not expire at the same time. The board of commissioners may provide for the appointment and compensation, if any, of alternate members to serve on the board in the absence of any regular member. Alternate members shall be appointed for the same term, at the same time, and in the same manner as regular members. Each alternate member, while attending any regular or special meeting of the board and serving in the absence of a regular member, has and may exercise all the powers and duties of a regular member. If the board of commissioners does not zone the entire territorial jurisdiction of the county, each designated zoning area shall have at least one resident as a member of the board of adjustment.

A county may designate a planning agency to perform any or all of the duties of a board of adjustment in addition to its other duties.

(b) The board of adjustment shall hear and decide appeals from and review any order, requirement, decision, or determination made by an administrative official charged with enforcing an ordinance adopted pursuant to this Part. Any person aggrieved or any officer, department, board, or bureau of the county may take an appeal. Appeals shall be taken within times prescribed by the board of adjustment by general rule, by filing with the officer from whom the appeal is taken and with the board of adjustment a notice of appeal, specifying the grounds thereof. The officer from whom the appeal is taken shall forthwith transmit to the board all the papers constituting the record upon which action appealed from was taken. An appeal stays all proceedings in furtherance of the action appealed from, unless the officer from whom the appeal is taken certifies to the board of adjustment, after notice of appeal has been filed with him, that because of facts stated in the certificate a stay would, in his opinion, cause imminent peril to life or property or that because the violation charged is transitory in nature a stay would seriously interfere with enforcement of the ordinance. In that case proceedings may not be stayed except by a restraining order, which may be granted by the board of adjustment or by a court of record on application, on notice to the officer from whom the appeal is taken and on due cause shown. The board of adjustment shall fix a reasonable time for the hearing of the appeal, give due notice of the appeal to the parties, and decide the appeal within a reasonable time. The board of adjustment may reverse or affirm, in whole or in part, or may modify the order, requirement, decision, or determination appealed from, and shall make any order, requirement, decision, or determination that in its opinion ought to be made in the circumstances. To this end the board has all of the powers of the officer from whom the appeal is taken.

(c) The zoning ordinance may provide that the board of adjustment may permit special exceptions to the zoning regulations in classes of cases or situations and in accordance with the principles, conditions, safeguards, and procedures specified in the ordinance. The ordinance may also authorize the board to interpret zoning maps and pass upon disputed questions of lot lines or district boundary lines and similar questions that may arise in the administration of the ordinance. The board shall hear and decide all matters referred to it or upon which it is required to pass under the zoning ordinance.

(d) When practical difficulties or unnecessary hardships would result from carrying out the strict letter of a zoning ordinance, the board of adjustment may, in passing upon appeals, vary or modify any regulation or provision of the ordinance relating to the use, construction, or alteration of buildings or structures or the use of land, so that the spirit of the ordinance is observed, public safety and welfare secured, and substantial justice done.

(e) The board of adjustment, by a vote of four-fifths of its members, may reverse any order, requirement, decision, or determination of an administrative officer charged with enforcing an ordinance adopted pursuant to this Part, or may decide in favor of the applicant a matter upon which the board is required to pass under the ordinance, or may grant a variance from the provisions of the ordinance. Each decision of the board is subject to review by the superior court by proceedings in the nature of certiorari. Any petition for review by the superior court shall be filed with the clerk of superior court within 30 days after the decision of the board is filed in such office as the ordinance specifies, or after a written copy thereof is delivered to every aggrieved party who has filed a written request for such copy with the secretary or chairman of the board at the time of its hearing of the case, whichever is later. The decision of the board may be delivered to the aggrieved party either by personal service or by registered mail or certified mail return receipt requested.

(f) The chairman of the board of adjustment or any member temporarily acting as chairman may in his official capacity administer oaths to witnesses in any matter coming before the board.

§ 153A-346. Conflict with other laws.

When regulations made under authority of this Part require a greater width or size of yards or courts, or require a lower height of a building or fewer number of stories, or require a greater percentage of a lot to be left unoccupied, or impose other higher standards than are required in any other statute or local ordinance or regulation, the regulations made under authority of this Part govern. When the provisions of any other statute or local ordinance or regulation require a greater width or size of yards or courts, or require a lower height of a building or a fewer number of stories, or require a greater percentage of a lot to be left unoccupied, or impose other higher standards than are required by regulations made under authority of this Part, the provisions of the other statute or local ordinance or regulation govern.

§ 153A-347. Part applicable to buildings constructed by the State and its subdivisions; exception.

Each provision of this Part is applicable to the erection, construction, and use of buildings by the State of North Carolina and its political subdivisions.

Notwithstanding the provisions of any general or local law or ordinance, no land owned by the State of North Carolina may be included within an overlay district or a special use or conditional use district without approval of the Council of State.

§ 153A-348. Statute of limitations.

A cause of action as to the validity of any zoning ordinance, or amendment thereto, adopted under this Part or other applicable law shall accrue upon adoption of the ordinance, or amendment thereto, and shall be brought within nine months as provided in G.S. 1-54.1.

Other Key Statutes

Cities

§ 160A-360. Territorial jurisdiction.

(a) All of the powers granted by this Article may be exercised by any city within its corporate limits. In addition, any city may exercise these powers within a defined area extending not more than one mile beyond its limits. With the approval of the board or boards of county commissioners with jurisdiction over the area, a city of 10,000 or more population but less than 25,000 may exercise these powers over an area extending not more than two miles beyond its limits and a city of 25,000 or more population may exercise these powers over an area extending not more than three miles beyond its limits. The boundaries of the city's extraterritorial jurisdiction shall be the same for all powers conferred in this Article. No city may exercise extraterritorially any power conferred by this Article that it is not exercising within its corporate limits. In determining the population of a city for the purposes of this Article, the city council and the board of county commissioners may use the most recent annual estimate of population as certified by the Secretary of the North Carolina Department of Administration.

(b) Any council wishing to exercise extraterritorial jurisdiction under this Article shall adopt, and may amend from time to time, an ordinance specifying the areas to be included based upon existing or projected urban development and areas of critical concern to the city, as evidenced by officially adopted plans for its development. Boundaries shall be defined, to the extent feasible, in terms of geographical features identifiable on the ground. A council may, in its discretion, exclude from its extraterritorial jurisdiction areas lying in another county, areas separated from the city by barriers to urban growth, or areas whose projected development will have minimal impact on the city. The boundaries specified in the ordinance shall at all times be drawn on a map, set forth in a written description, or shown by a combination of these techniques. This delineation shall be maintained in the manner provided in G.S. 160A-22 for the delineation of the corporate limits, and shall be recorded in the office of the register of deeds of each county in which any portion of the area lies.

(c) Where the extraterritorial jurisdiction of two or more cities overlaps, the jurisdictional boundary between them shall be a line connecting the midway points of the overlapping area unless the city councils agree to another boundary line within the overlapping area based upon existing or projected patterns of development.

(d) If a city fails to adopt an ordinance specifying the boundaries of its extraterritorial jurisdiction, the county of which it is a part shall be authorized to exercise the powers granted by this Article in any area beyond the city's corporate limits. The county may also, on request of the city council, exercise any or all these powers in any or all areas lying within the city's corporate limits or within the city's specified area of extraterritorial jurisdiction.

(e) No city may hereafter extend its extraterritorial powers under this Article into any area for which the county at that time has adopted and is enforcing a zoning ordinance and subdivision regulations and within which it is enforcing the State Building Code. However, the city may do so where the county is not exercising all three of these powers, or when the city and the county have agreed upon the area within which each will exercise the powers conferred by this Article.

(f) When a city annexes, or a new city is incorporated in, or a city extends its jurisdiction to include, an area that is currently being regulated by the county, the county regulations and powers of enforcement shall remain in effect until (i) the city has adopted such regulations, or (ii) a period of 60 days has elapsed following the annexation, extension or incorporation, whichever is sooner. During this period the city may hold hearings and take any other measures that may be required in order to adopt its regulations for the area.

(f1) When a city relinquishes jurisdiction over an area that it is regulating under this Article to a county, the city regulations and powers of enforcement shall remain in effect until (i) the county has adopted this regulation or (ii) a period of 60 days has elapsed following the action by which the city relinquished jurisdiction, whichever is sooner. During this period the county may hold hearings and take other measures that may be required in order to adopt its regulations for the area.

(g) When a local government is granted powers by this section subject to the request, approval, or agreement of another local government, the request, approval, or agreement shall be evidenced by a formally adopted resolution of that government's legislative body. Any such request, approval, or agreement can be rescinded upon two years' written notice to the other legislative bodies concerned by repealing the resolution. The resolution may be modified at any time by mutual agreement of the legislative bodies concerned.

(h) Nothing in this section shall repeal, modify, or amend any local act which defines the boundaries of a city's extraterritorial jurisdiction by metes and bounds or courses and distances.

(i) Whenever a city or county, pursuant to this section, acquires jurisdiction over a territory that theretofore has been subject to the jurisdiction of another local government, any person who has acquired vested rights under a permit, certificate, or other evidence of compliance issued by the local government surrendering jurisdiction may exercise those rights as if no change of jurisdiction had occurred. The city or county acquiring jurisdiction may take any action regarding such a permit, certificate, or other

evidence of compliance that could have been taken by the local government surrendering jurisdiction pursuant to its ordinances and regulations.
Except as provided in this subsection, any building, structure, or other
land use in a territory over which a city or county has acquired jurisdiction
is subject to the ordinances and regulations of the city or county.

(j) Repealed by Session Laws 1973, c. 669, s. 1.

§ 160A-361. Planning agency.

Any city may by ordinance create or designate one or more agencies
to perform the following duties:

(1) Make studies of the area within its jurisdiction and surrounding
areas;

(2) Determine objectives to be sought in the development of the study
area;

(3) Prepare and adopt plans for achieving these objectives;

(4) Develop and recommend policies, ordinances, administrative procedures, and other means for carrying out plans in a coordinated and efficient manner;

(5) Advise the council concerning the use and amendment of means
for carrying out plans;

(6) Exercise any functions in the administration and enforcement of
various means for carrying out plans that the council may direct;

(7) Perform any other related duties that the council may direct.

An agency created or designated pursuant to this section may include,
but shall not be limited to, one or more of the following, with such staff
as the council may deem appropriate:

(1) A planning board or commission of any size (not less than three
members) or composition deemed appropriate, organized in any manner
deemed appropriate;

(2) A joint planning board created by two or more local governments
pursuant to Article 20, Part 1, of this Chapter.

§ 160A-362. Extraterritorial representation.

When a city elects to exercise extraterritorial zoning or subdivision-
regulation powers under G.S. 160A-360, it shall in the ordinance creating or designating its planning agency or agencies provide a means of
representation for residents of the extraterritorial area to be regulated.
Representation shall be provided by appointing residents of the area to
the planning agency and the board of adjustment that makes recommendations or grants relief in these matters. Any advisory board established prior to July 1, 1983, to provide the required extraterritorial representation shall constitute compliance with this section until the board
is abolished by ordinance of the city. The representatives on the planning

agency and the board of adjustment shall be appointed by the board of county commissioners with jurisdiction over the area. If there is an insufficient number of qualified residents of the area to meet membership requirements, the board of county commissioners may appoint as many other residents of the county as necessary to make up the requisite number. When the extraterritorial area extends into two or more counties, each board of county commissioners concerned shall appoint representatives from its portion of the area, as specified in the ordinance. If a board of county commissioners fails to make these appointments within 90 days after receiving a resolution from the city council requesting that they be made, the city council may make them. If the ordinance so provides, the outside representatives may have equal rights, privileges, and duties with the other members of the agency to which they are appointed, regardless of whether the matters at issue arise within the city or within the extraterritorial area; otherwise they shall function only with respect to matters within the extraterritorial area.

§ 160A-364. Procedure for adopting or amending ordinances under Article.

Before adopting or amending any ordinance authorized by this Article, the city council shall hold a public hearing on it. A notice of the public hearing shall be given once a week for two successive calendar weeks in a newspaper having general circulation in the area. The notice shall be published the first time not less than 10 days nor more than 25 days before the date fixed for the hearing. In computing such period, the day of publication is not to be included but the day of the hearing shall be included.

§ 160A-364.1. Statute of limitations.

A cause of action as to the validity of any zoning ordinance, or amendment thereto, adopted under this Article or other applicable law shall accrue upon adoption of the ordinance, or amendment thereto, and shall be brought within nine months as provided in G.S. 1-54.1.

Counties

§ 153A-320. Territorial jurisdiction.

Each of the powers granted to counties by this Article, by Chapter 157A, and by Chapter 160A, Article 19 may be exercised throughout the county except as otherwise provided in G.S. 160A-360.

§ 153A-321. Planning agency.

A county may by ordinance create or designate one or more agencies to perform the following duties:

(1) Make studies of the county and surrounding areas;

(2) Determine objectives to be sought in the development of the study area;

(3) Prepare and adopt plans for achieving these objectives;

(4) Develop and recommend policies, ordinances, administrative procedures, and other means for carrying out plans in a coordinated and efficient manner;

(5) Advise the board of commissioners concerning the use and amendment of means for carrying out plans;

(6) Exercise any functions in the administration and enforcement of various means for carrying out plans that the board of commissioners may direct;

(7) Perform any other related duties that the board of commissioners may direct.

An agency created or designated pursuant to this section may include but shall not be limited to one or more of the following, with any staff that the board of commissioners considers appropriate:

(1) A planning board or commission of any size (not less than three members) or composition considered appropriate, organized in any manner considered appropriate;

(2) A joint planning board created by two or more local governments according to the procedures and provisions of Chapter 160A, Article 20, Part 1.

§ 153A-323. Procedure for adopting or amending ordinances under this Article and Chapter 160A, Article 19.

Before adopting or amending any ordinance authorized by this Article or Chapter 160A, Article 19, the board of commissioners shall hold a public hearing on the ordinance or amendment. The board shall cause notice of the hearing to be published once a week for two successive calendar weeks. The notice shall be published the first time not less than 10 days nor more than 25 days before the date fixed for the hearing. In computing such period, the day of publication is not to be included but the day of the hearing shall be included.

Appendix 2: Further References on North Carolina Zoning Law

References listed below are published by the Institute of Government of The University of North Carolina at Chapel Hill.

Books

Brough, Michael B., and Philip P. Green, Jr. *The Zoning Board of Adjustment in North Carolina.* 2d ed. Institute of Government, 1984.

Ducker, Richard D. *Subdivision Regulations in North Carolina: An Introduction.* Institute of Government, 1980.

Green, Philip P., Jr. *Legal Responsibilities of the Local Zoning Administrator in North Carolina.* 2d ed. Institute of Government, 1987.

Green, Philip P., Jr. *Organizing for Local Government Planning in North Carolina.* Institute of Government, 1989.

Lawrence, David M. *Open Meetings and Local Governments in North Carolina: Some Questions and Answers.* Institute of Government, 1994.

Owens, David W. *Conflicts of Interest in Land-Use Management Decisions.* Institute of Government, 1990.

Owens, David W. *Planning Legislation in North Carolina.* Institute of Government, 1991.

Owens, David W. *Legislative Zoning Decisions: Legal Aspects.* Institute of Government, 1993.

Articles

Ducker, Richard D. "Administering Subdivision Ordinances." *Popular Government* 45 (Summer 1979): 20–28.

Ducker, Richard D. "Federal and State Programs to Control Signs and Outdoor Advertising." *Popular Government* 52 (Spring 1987): 28–42.

Ducker, Richard D. "Land Use Planning in Rural Areas." *Popular Government* 46 (Summer 1980): 28–34.

Ducker, Richard D. "Off-street Parking in North Carolina Municipalities." *Popular Government* 46 (Summer 1980): 39–42.

Ducker, Richard D. "Using Impact Fees for Public Schools." *School Law Bulletin* (Spring 1994): 1–13.

Green, Philip P., Jr. "Questions I'm Most Often Asked: What is 'Spot Zoning?'" *Popular Government* 51 (Summer 1985): 50–53.

Owens, David W. "Amortization: An Old Land-Use Controversy Heats Up." *Popular Government* 57 (Fall 1991): 20–29.

Owens, David W. "Bias and Conflicts of Interest in Land-Use Management Decisions." *Popular Government* 55 (Winter 1990): 29–36.

Owens, David W. "Land Use and Development Moratoria." *Popular Government* 56 (Fall 1990): 31–36.

Owens, David W. "Zoning Hearings: Knowing Which Rules to Apply." *Popular Government* 58 (Spring 1993): 26–35.

Bulletins

Bell, A. Fleming, II. "Telling the Neighbors What You Think: *City of Ladue v. Gilleo*." *Local Government Law Bulletin*, no. 61, August 1994.

Ducker, Richard D. "'Taking' Found for Beach Access Dedication Requirement: *Nolan v. California Coastal Commission*." *Local Government Law Bulletin*, no. 30, August 1987.

Green, Philip P., Jr. "Temporary Damages for a Regulatory 'Taking': *First English Evangelical Lutheran Church v. County of Los Angeles*." *Local Government Law Bulletin*, no. 29, July 1987.

Green, Philip P., Jr. "Two Major Zoning Decisions: *Chrismon v. Guilford County* and *Hall v. City of Durham*." *Local Government Law Bulletin*, no. 34, November 1988.

Owens, David W., Richard D. Ducker, and Milton S. Heath, Jr. "Supreme Court Establishes Rule on 'Total Taking': Perspectives on the *Lucas* Case." *Planning and Zoning Law Bulletin,* no. 3, September 1992.

Index

Adult entertainment, 76–77
Advertisement, 36–37
Advisory zoning decisions, 30, 57
Agriculture, 83, 101
Alcohol, 83–84
Amortization, 71, 72, 81–82
Annexation, 13–14
Appeals, 57
Applications, 61
Aydlett case, 6–10

Board of Adjustment, 33, 49, 98–
    100, 109–11
Building permit, 69–70

Chrismon case, 44–45
City jurisdiction, 13–14
Compensation, 77–82
Comprehensive plan, 41–42, 43
Conditional-use districts, 23, 44–
    46
Conditional-use permits, 24–25,
    54–55, 89, 101
Conflict of interest, 51, 74
Contract zoning, 44–46
County jurisdiction, 14, 102–3,
    115
Cumulative districts, 19–20, 22

Dedications, 82
Delegation, 4
Dimensional requirements, 25–27
Districts, 4, 19–24, 90, 102–3
Due process, 73–75

Enforcement, 60–65, 100
Equal protection, 75–76
Evidentiary hearings, 31

Exactions, 82
Ex parte communication, 50
Extraterritorial jurisdiction, 14–18,
    112–14

Fair Housing Act, 84
Family-care homes, 84
Farms, 83, 100
Fifth Amendment, 77–78
Finch case, 79–81
Findings of fact, 51
First Amendment, 76–77
Floating districts, 23–24
Flood hazards, 22, 27
Fourteenth Amendment, 73–76

Hardship, 56
Hearings, 30–31, 37–38
Hearsay, 50
Historic preservation, 28, 85
History of zoning, 5–11
Housing codes, 11
Humble Oil case, 52–54

Interlocal agreements, 18

Joyner case, 72
Judicial review, 46–47, 57–58
Jurisdiction, 13–18, 112–14

Landscaping, 27
Land-use plans, 41–42
Legislative zoning decisions, 29,
    35–47

Mailed notice, 36–37
Manufactured housing, 85–86,
    90, 102

Minutes, 32, 34, 51
Mobile homes, 85–86
Motive of governing board in
   making decisions, 38
Multiple-use districts, 24

Neotraditional development, 24
Nonconformities, 70–72
Notice, 36–37, 91–92, 103, 115,
   116

Oaths, 50, 59
Officers, 59
Open meetings, 33–34, 51
Overlay zones, 22

Permitted uses, 24
Plan, 41–42
Planned unit development, 24
Planning board, 32, 97–98, 104,
   114–15, 116
Protest petitions, 38–41, 92–93, 97
Public buildings, 86, 101, 111
Public hearings, 30–31, 37–40
Public records, 34, 60
Purposes of zoning, 4, 74, 89, 90,
   101–2

Quasi-judicial zoning decisions,
   29–30, 49–58

Record keeping, 51, 60

Rehearing, 39–40, 52
Religion, freedom of, 77
Restrictive covenants, 10, 12
Rezoning, 19, 35–47

Satellite dishes, 86
Search warrant, 61–62
Sign regulations, 27, 77
Site-specific development plan,
   68, 70, 93–97, 105–9
Special-use permits, 24–25, 54–
   55, 89, 101
Speech, zoning and freedom of,
   76–77
Spot zoning, 42–44
State-local relations, 4, 10–11
Stop work order, 63–64
Subdivisions, 11
Substantial expenditure, 69

Taking, 77–82

Use by right, 24
Use districts, 19–24
Use restrictions, 24–25

Variance, 55–57, 99, 111
Vested rights, 67–70
Voting, 38–39, 52, 89, 99, 110

Waiting periods, 39–40
Watersheds, 86–87